Complete Library Skills

Grade 4

Published by Instructional Fair
an imprint of

McGraw Hill **Children's Publishing**

Author: Linda Turrell
Editor: Cary Malaski

Published by Instructional Fair
An imprint of McGraw-Hill Children's Publishing
Copyright © 2004 McGraw-Hill Children's Publishing

*The Dewey Decimal Classification System is a registered trademark of Forest Press, Inc.

Send all inquiries to:
McGraw-Hill Children's Publishing
3195 Wilson Drive NW
Grand Rapids, Michigan 49544

Complete Library Skills—grade 4
ISBN: 0-7424-1954-1

1 2 3 4 5 6 7 8 9 MAZ 09 08 07 06 05 04
The *McGraw-Hill* Companies

Table of Contents

Name _____   Date _____

Fiction and Nonfiction

Do you know the difference between fiction and nonfiction? In order to find books quickly and easily, you need to know the difference between these two categories. Your library has an entire section of books that are **fiction**. These are all shelved together. You will find them easily because their call numbers are in alphabetical order. You can find what you need by looking for the letter *F* and then the first two letters of the author's last name. The letter *F* stands for *fiction*—books that have made-up or imaginary stories.

Nonfiction books are also grouped in one section of the library. They usually contain information about different subjects, such as science, history, geography, or languages. These types of books are factual—they describe true facts and events about the topic being written about. There are many kinds of nonfiction books. In nonfiction books, you can learn about foreign countries, famous people, volcanic eruptions, or growing an herb garden. These books are arranged numerically according to the subject matter.

Compare these two titles—*Inside a Volcano* and *Attack of the Red Hot Lava*. Which book do you think is true? *Inside a Volcano* describes the physical features of the inside of a volcano, so it is a nonfiction book. Does *Attack of the Red Hot Lava* sound real or made-up? It is a made-up story, so it is fiction.

► **In your library, find fiction and nonfiction books. Write the titles and authors below.**

Fiction

_____

_____

_____

_____

Nonfiction

_____

_____

_____

_____

Name _____   Date _____

Your Favorite Book

➤ **Illustrate the cover of your favorite fiction or nonfiction book. Include a title and the author's name with your drawing.**

True or Made-Up?

➤ **Read each book title and description below. Write fiction or nonfiction on the line.**

1. *A Helping Hen* by Amy Wimble. This is the story of a hen who helps an entire town survive. _____

2. *The Giant Beehive* by Pamela Poof. This is the story of a woman with a ten-foot hairstyle. _____

3. *Prehistoric Times* by Guy Matson. This book describes Earth during the dinosaur age. _____

4. *Training Spot* by Roy Buggs. This book features the latest techniques for training dogs. _____

5. *Building Your Own Deck* by Dan Purmus. This book includes directions and plans for building ten different types of decks. _____

6. *Sports Legends* by William Teems. This book describes the lives of famous sports stars such as Jackie Robinson, Jack Nicklaus, Billie Jean King, and more. _____

7. *My Life as a Pilot* by Matthew Fremont. This is an autobiography of a stunt pilot. _____

8. *The Friendly Toaster* by Mike Burn. This book is about a toaster who makes toast with a smile. _____

9. *The Empty Safe* by Caren Parker. This book is about one of the largest jewel heists of all time. _____

10. *Packing for a Trip* by John Barker. This book gives advice on packing for a vacation. _____

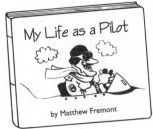

Name _____ Date _____

Fiction Call Numbers

Books have "addresses" just like houses do. The call number helps you find a book quickly and easily. A book's address is called its **call number**, and it helps people find it on a bookshelf. The call number can be found on the book's spine.

A fiction book has an *F*, for fiction, on its spine above the call number. Fiction call numbers are the first two letters of the author's last name. Fiction books are placed on bookshelves in alphabetical order by their call numbers.

▶ **Look at the examples below.**

1. Jeff Carpenter wrote *Fudge-A-Rama*, a fiction book. If you weren't sure if it was fiction or not, you could look at the spine for an F. What two letters would you find under the F? Write them on the book spine.

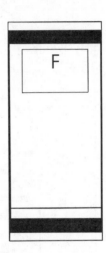

2. *My Night on Pluto* was written by Fawn Faraway. It is a fiction book. What two letters make up its call number? Write them on the spine.

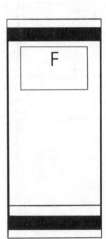

3. On the book spine, write the call number for the book titled *Call of the Wild* by John Stuckey.

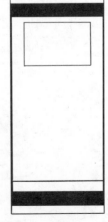

Don't Miss This Call

Call numbers help you find books on bookshelves. If books didn't have call numbers, you wouldn't know where to start looking for a specific book.

Look at the books below. They are all fiction. For each book, write its call number on the spine next to it. Don't forget to start each call number with an *F* for fiction.

1.

2.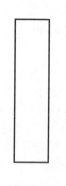

3.

4.

5.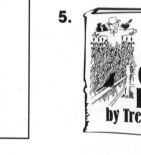

6.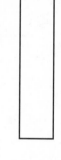

7.

8.

9.

Name _____ Date _____

Order Up!

When you look at fiction books on bookshelves, you will notice they are in a certain order. Fiction books are arranged according to the first two letters of the author's last name.

► **Look at the fiction call numbers on the left. Draw a line to match each call number on the left to the author who wrote the book on the right. Then write the authors' names in alphabetical order on the lines. This is the order you would find them in on the bookshelves.**

1. F Ba	**a.** Roger Snider	_____
2. F Zu	**b.** Greg Phent	_____
3. F Ra	**c.** Tania Rabinau	_____
4. F Ob	**d.** Jennifer Filey	_____
5. F Sn	**e.** Bob Dilbert	_____
6. F Ro	**f.** Aaron Brody	_____
7. F Di	**g.** Cho Obo	_____
8. F Br	**h.** Henry Rolston	_____
9. F Po	**i.** Catherine Marks	_____
10. F Ma	**j.** Barbara White	_____
11. F Cr	**k.** Clint Hubbert	_____
12. F Wh	**l.** Todd Bally	_____
13. F Ph	**m.** Dan Porter	_____
14. F Hu	**n.** Lindsey Crowley	_____
15. F Fi	**o.** Carrie Zucker	_____

Musical Books

The alphabet can be divided into three sections—A–H, I–Q, and R–Z. These three sections make up the beginning, middle, and end of the alphabet. When looking for a book on the bookshelf, it helps to know which section of the alphabet the book can be found in.

➡ **Look at the fiction books below. Fiction books are arranged in alphabetical order on bookshelves by the first two letters of the author's last name. Look at the author's last name and decide which section of the alphabet the book is in. Write the authors' names in the correct sections below.**

Book Titles and Authors

The Longest Night by Sherry Thomson

Henrietta, the Harry Hippo by Helen Haward

My Dog the Spy by Adrienne Armor

The Mystery of the Chocolate Cake by Brent Buster

The Ground Is Caving In! by Sarah Jackson

My Life as an International Zookeeper by Alison Martin

I Didn't Know Any Better! by Trent Wilson

The Disappearing Campground by Amy Pilson

The Purple Sticky Note, Part 1 by Susan White

Attack of the Angry Scissors by Paul Peterson

You Want to Go Where? by Fran Henderson

Beginning	Middle	End

Nonfiction Call Numbers

Nonfiction books have their own section of the library. They are about all different subjects, such as energy, outer space, people, and machines. Folktales, fairy tales, and poetry are all considered nonfiction.

Like a fiction book, a nonfiction book also has an "address" on its spine that helps you find it on the bookshelf. It is easy to tell the difference between a fiction and a nonfiction book because the nonfiction book has numbers as well as letters (fiction books just have letters). These numbers and letters make up its call number. The numbers on the spine of a nonfiction book are part of the Dewey Decimal Classification® system. This is a system of organizing books according to the subjects they are about. It begins with 000 and ends with 999. You will learn more about this system later in the book.

The book titled *The Book of Sculptures* by Ann Platt has a call number of:

730
Pl

Section of the library

Ann Platt

The Complete Book of Spanish Words by Michael Coad has a call number of:

460
Co

Section of the library

Michael Coad

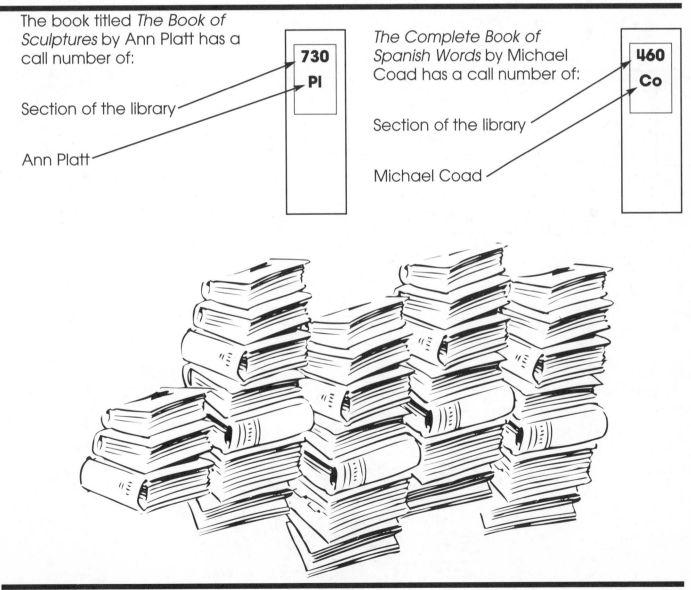

Name _____ Date _____

How Nonfiction Books Are Arranged

Since nonfiction books have both letters and numbers as part of the call numbers, they are arranged a little differently than fiction books. They are first arranged on bookshelves according to their three-digit numbers. They are arranged starting with the lowest call number (000) up to the highest call number (999). Look at the bookshelf below. These nonfiction books are in order.

127 Po	230 Za	310 Wa	420 St	589 Va	636 Ma	707 Ch	801 Fi	950 Br

Sometimes more than one book can have the same three-digit number in its call number. When this happens, the books are arranged alphabetically by the author's last name. Look at the bookshelf below. These nonfiction books are in order, also.

580 Ma	580 Za	616 Th	616 Wh	798 Aa	798 Va	810 Di	810 Ja	810 Nu

▶ **Rearrange the following nonfiction call numbers so that they are in order. Write 1–8 under the call numbers.**

785 Po	991 Ma	231 Ba	231 Du	129 Ru	555 St	991 Al	382 Ri

_____   _____   _____   _____   _____   _____   _____   _____

Name _____ Date _____

Arrange the Nonfiction Books

▶ **Put the following nonfiction call numbers in order. Remember that if two or more call numbers have the same numbers, you have to look at the letters and arrange them alphabetically. Number them 1–5.**

1.

400 Ta	800 Bl	900 Br	600 St	300 Ad

2.

400 Wa	600 Re	500 Al	300 Sr	200 Be

3.

900 De	700 Fl	500 Ho	400 Jo	200 Cr

4.

470 Sr	470 Bu	450 Fr	420 Fl	410 Ma

5.

850 Th	890 Bu	890 Ze	830 Gu	870 Me

Name _____   Date _____

Whale of a Trail

Nonfiction books are arranged on bookshelves first in numerical order by the three-digit call number. Then, if two or more books have the same three-digit call number, they are arranged alphabetically by the first two letters of the author's last name.

Look at the examples below.

Out of order: 150 Ba   220 Tu   150 Ma

In order: 150 Ba   150 Ma   220 Tu

▶ **Follow the trail in the order that the books would appear on the bookshelf.**

190 Ba   240 Aa   220 Su

200 Zu

280 Ch   330 Th   350 Tr

110 Mo

970 Os   310 Ew

520 Cr   470 Va   470 Pu   400 Hi

690 Du   550 Rh   470 Br

780 Ar   760 Ja   390 Wh   140 Bo   880 Bi   870 Ki

780 St   840 Kl   840 Bl   990 Jo

660 Ma   900 Ma

Name _____ Date _____

Understanding the Card Catalog

The card catalog contains cards of information about every book in the library. Each book has three cards of information—one for the author, title, and subject of the book.

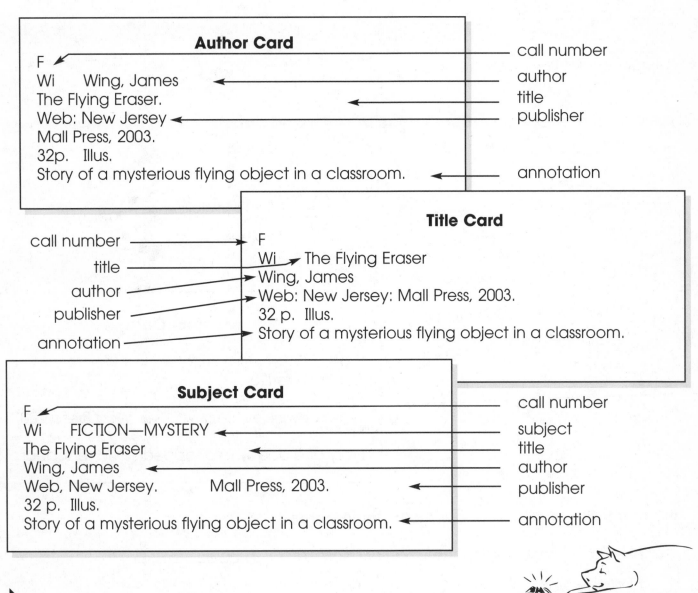

Author Card

F ← call number
Wi   Wing, James ← author
The Flying Eraser. ← title
Web: New Jersey ← publisher
Mall Press, 2003.
32p. Illus.
Story of a mysterious flying object in a classroom. ← annotation

Title Card

call number →
title →
author →
publisher →
annotation →

F
Wi → The Flying Eraser
Wing, James
Web: New Jersey: Mall Press, 2003.
32 p. Illus.
Story of a mysterious flying object in a classroom.

Subject Card

F ← call number
Wi   FICTION—MYSTERY ← subject
The Flying Eraser ← title
Wing, James ← author
Web, New Jersey.   Mall Press, 2003. ← publisher
32 p. Illus.
Story of a mysterious flying object in a classroom. ← annotation

▶ **Answer the questions below.**

1. Which type of card would you use if you wanted a book about **earthquakes**, but you didn't know the title or author of a specific book? _____

2. Which type of card would you use if you wanted to find *Charlotte's Web*, but you didn't know the author's name? _____

Name _____ Date _____

Card Catalog Drawers

A card catalog is made up of three drawers—subject, title, and author. The cards in each drawer show you the call number, author, title, publisher, place of publication, copyright date, page count, and a short summary of the book. They can also show you if the book has illustrations.

Look at the three cards below.

Author Card

F
Po   Porter, Jeff
The Disappearing Tire Tracks.
Screech: New Jersey
Peel Press, 2003.
68p.   Illus.
Story of mysterious tire tracks that disappear.

Title Card

F
Ha   The Haunted Old Clock
Hand, Susan
Chime, New York: Watch Press, 2003.
101 p.   Illus.
Story of a haunted clock.

Subject Card

F
Wo   FICTION—MYSTERY
The Invisible Dog
Woof, Robert
Waterbowl, New Jersey.   Wag Press, 2003.
65 p. Illus.
Story of a dog who disappears and reappears.

▶ **Answer the questions about the catalog cards.**

1. Is *The Haunted Old Clock* fiction or nonfiction? _____

2. Where was *The Invisible Dog* published? _____

3. How many pages does *The Disappearing Tire Tracks* have? _____

4. Which book is the shortest? _____

5. On the top line of each card, what type of information is the same? _____

6. If you wanted to find a mystery, which catalog drawer would you use? _____

Name _____ Date _____

Reading a Card

▶ **Look at the card below. Answer the questions.**

```
F
Pl   Nick Nederveld, Ping-Pong Superstar
Platts, Pamela
New York, New York: Volley Press, 2003.
54 p.  Illus.
Story of a table-tennis champion.
```

1. What is the call number? _____

2. What is the title? _____

3. Who is the author? _____

4. Where was the book published? _____

5. Who published the book? _____

6. What year was the book made (copyright date)? _____

7. Does the book have illustrations? _____

8. What is the book about? _____

9. Is the book fiction or nonfiction? _____

10. What type of card is this? _____

Reading a Card

▶ **Look at the card below. Answer the questions.**

F
Th   Thompson, Mitch
The Overprotective Watchdog.
Rockville: New Jersey.
Valley Press, 2003.
80 p. Illus.
The story of an overprotective dog.

1. What is the call number? _____

2. What is the title? _____

3. Who is the author? _____

4. How many pages does this book have? _____

5. What is this book about? _____

6. Where was this book published? _____

7. Is this book fiction or nonfiction? _____

8. Does this book have illustrations? _____

9. What year was this book published (copyright date)? _____

10. Who published the book? _____

Reading a Card

Look at the card below. Answer the questions.

1. What is the title? _____

2. What is the call number? _____

3. Is this book fiction or nonfiction? _____

4. Who is the author? _____

5. How many pages does this book have? _____

6. When was this book published (copyright date)? _____

7. What is this book about? _____

8. Does this book have illustrations? _____

9. What is the subject of this book? _____

10. What type of card is this? _____

> F
> FI   FICTION—FEELINGS
> The New Kid
> Flann, James
> Chester, New York.
> Dove Press, 2003.
> 45 p. Illus.
> Story of a boy who just moved to a new town.

Write Your Own Card

➤ **Write a card for one of your favorite books. Include the following information—Call number, Title, Author, Place of Publication, Publisher, Copyright Date, Pages, Illustrated (or not), and Annotation (summary of book). Make sure you decide which type of card you are writing before you start.**

Call number

Title

Author and Title

Place of Publication, Publisher, Copyright Date

Pages

Illustrated or not

Sentence describing what the book is about.

What type of card did you just write? _____

Name _____ Date _____

A Book Divided

Dictionaries are made up of three sections—A–H, I–Q, and R–Z. Using these sections makes finding words in a dictionary easier.

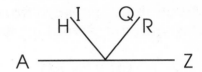

► **Using a dictionary, find five words that can be found in each of the three sections of the dictionary. Write them in the correct box below.**

A–H	I–Q	R–Z
_____	_____	_____
_____	_____	_____
_____	_____	_____
_____	_____	_____
_____	_____	_____

Dictionaries have guide words at the top of every page. These words tell you the first and last words on each page. They help guide you to the words on that page.

Open your dictionary to a middle page.

On what page are you? _____

What are the guide words on this page? _____ and _____

Would the word *mustard* come before, on, or after this page? _____

Open your dictionary to a beginning page.

On what page are you? _____

What are the guide words on this page? _____ and _____

Would the word *deliberate* come before, on, or after this page? _____

Open your dictionary to an end page.

On what page are you? _____

What are the guide words on this page? _____ and _____

Would the word *venture* come before, on, or after this page? _____

Name _____ Date _____

An Egyptian Journey

► **Match the entry word from the Word Bank to the correct guide words. Write the entry word on the line.**

Entry Word	Guide Words	Word Bank
1. _____	depart–detour	pharaoh
2. _____	pineapple–python	ancient
3. _____	sailboat–second	pyramid
4. _____	anchor–ankle	desert
5. _____	peanut–picnic	sand

► **Use a dictionary to find the guide words for the words below.**

Entry Word   **Guide Words**

archaeologists   _____ and _____

mummy   _____ and _____

sphinx   _____ and _____

curse   _____ and _____

treasure   _____ and _____

Egyptian   _____ and _____

tomb   _____ and _____

jewels   _____ and _____

► **Using both lists of entry words above and the clues below telling where the words are found in the dictionary, complete the story.**

King Tut became a _____ when he was only nine years old. Like other
                          middle

_____ _____ kings, his _____ lies in a
     beginning   beginning   end

_____. In 1922, a team of _____ found King Tut's
     beginning   beginning

_____ and the _____ surrounding it. This discovery in the
     middle   end

desert _____ was both magnificent and mysterious. Along with the
           end

_____ , a deadly _____ was uncovered. Twenty people
     middle   beginning

associated with the dig mysteriously died soon after the tomb was opened.

Name _____ Date _____

Snake Eyes

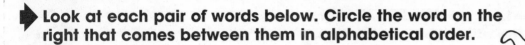

► **Look at each pair of words below. Circle the word on the right that comes between them in alphabetical order.**

1. girl _____ jockey	indoor	party	ghost
2. mighty _____ nook	mail	midnight	neat
3. safe _____ soon	soccer	sack	sore
4. cold _____ count	canopy	court	copy
5. white _____ wink	winter	wig	whistle
6. feather _____ filling	fender	famous	fish
7. ocean _____ other	oatmeal	over	orphan
8. program _____ put	prime	push	peas
9. king _____ know	kiss	kind	knowledge
10. yawn _____ young	zero	yarn	year
11. hungry _____ hurry	hush	hurtle	hunter
12. reward _____ ripe	ripple	right	review
13. promise _____ proud	prose	pride	profit
14. basket _____ baste	busy	basic	bass
15. life _____ ligament	line	legal	lift

► **Cross out the words that do not fall in alphabetical order between the given words. Read the remaining words to learn an interesting snake fact.**

sloppy-solar	happen-hay	nitrogen-normal	east-eyeliner
spear	half	never	feet
sleep	have	notable	ears
slither	help	nine	eyes
snakes	hide	now	eyelids
sheep	hand	no	fingers

What did you learn about snakes? _____

Guide to the Stars

▶ **Match the entry words in the Word Bank to the correct guide words. Write the entry word on the line.**

Entry Word	**Guide Words**
1. _____	telecast–telethon
2. _____	stanza–stately
3. _____	lieutenant–lilac
4. _____	skipper–slate
5. _____	pictorial–pigmentation
6. _____	souvenir–spaghetti
7. _____	assuage–asylum

Word Bank

light

space

telescope

astronomy

sky

picture

star

▶ **Trace the starlit path of entry words in the order of your answers above. You will see a well-known constellation.**

star

jet

astronaut

telescope

light

meteor

astronomy

space

sky

moon

astronomer

space

picture

starlight

shuttle

Name _____ Date _____

Di•vi•ding Words

➤ On the lines below, write the words showing where they are divided into syllables. Use a • to divide the word into syllables. Then check your answers in a dictionary. Write the number of syllables in each word in the parentheses.

triangle	**puzzle**	**grape**
_____ ( )	_____ ( )	_____ ( )

millionaire	**television**	**train**
_____ ( )	_____ ( )	_____ ( )

arithmetic	**feather**	**candle**
_____ ( )	_____ ( )	_____ ( )

dolphin	**caterpillar**	**lion**
_____ ( )	_____ ( )	_____ ( )

Did You Know? Mary Poppins created the word supercalifragilisticexpialidocious.

Can you divide this word into syllables?

_____

How many syllables does it have? _____

Can you find this word in the dictionary? _____

Decisions, Decisions

➤ **Circle the choice that shows the correct division of each word. If you get stuck, you know where to find the answers—in your dictionary!**

1. dragonfly	drag•on•fly	dra•gon•fly	
2. doughnut	dou•ghnut	dough•nut	
3. radio	ra•dio	ra•di•o	
4. poem	po•em	poem	
5. praise	praise	prai•se	
6. responsible	res•pons•i•ble	re•spon•si•ble	
7. letter	lett•er	let•ter	
8. oxygen	ox•y•gen	ox•yg•en	
9. journal	jour•nal	journ•al	

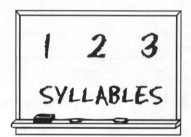

➤ **Using a dictionary, write the guide words for the following words. Then write the words using a • to show the syllables.**

Word	Guide Words	Syllables
10. consistent	_____ and _____	_____
11. dehydration	_____ and _____	_____
12. terrible	_____ and _____	_____
13. avenue	_____ and _____	_____
14. unwind	_____ and _____	_____
15. endeavor	_____ and _____	_____
16. uniform	_____ and _____	_____
17. category	_____ and _____	_____
18. conscious	_____ and _____	_____
19. grandson	_____ and _____	_____

Riddle: What is one behavior apes show? Write the first letter of the second syllable of each word above to answer the riddle.

___ ___ ___ ___ ___ ___ ___ ___ ___ ___

Name _____ Date _____

What Kind of Word Is It?

▶ **Identify the correct part of speech for each underlined word. Use the dictionary entries for help.**

chime /'chīm/ **n.** 1. A set of bells. 2. The sound of bells **v.** 1. To make a musical sound

slick /'slĭk/ **n.** 1. Something that is slippery 2. A film of oil **v.** 1. To make smooth or slippery **adj.** 1. Slippery 2. Clever

yellow /'yĕl ō/ **n.** 1. A color like a lemon **v.** 1. To become yellow **adj.** 1. Of the color yellow 2. Cowardly

Noun, Verb, or Adjective

1. Mary rang the <u>chimes</u> for dinner at six o'clock. _____

2. I sat in a <u>yellow</u> chair in the doctor's office. _____

3. We walked carefully because the sidewalk was <u>slick</u> after the rain. _____

4. Angella <u>slicked</u> back her hair for the school play. _____

5. A green banana will be <u>yellow</u> in only a few days. _____

6. Mr. Leatherby heard the <u>chime</u> sounding in the wind. _____

▶ **Write the word from the Word Bank that best completes each sentence. Using your dictionary, write the page number in the ( ) to show where you found the word.**

7. The boat stopped with a _____( ) when it hit the large rock.

8. Each night I could see the new moon _____( ) until I beheld a beautiful full moon.

9. The dog had a thorn in the _____( ) of its foot.

10. As the flood waters began to _____( ), the rescuers could see the damage from the storm.

11. Lucy's parents said she could keep the _____( ) as a pet if no one claimed it.

Word Bank

wax

pad

jolt

stray

ebb

Name _____   Date _____

Where Does It Belong?

▶ **Look at the words in the Word Bank. Use a dictionary to figure out if the words are nouns, verbs, or both. Write the nouns in the noun section of the Venn diagram. Write the verbs in the verb section of the diagram. If a word is both a noun and a verb, write the word in the overlapping section of the diagram.**

Word Bank

keep	restaurant	decide	produce
maze	flip	soda	match
publish	copy	plant	carry

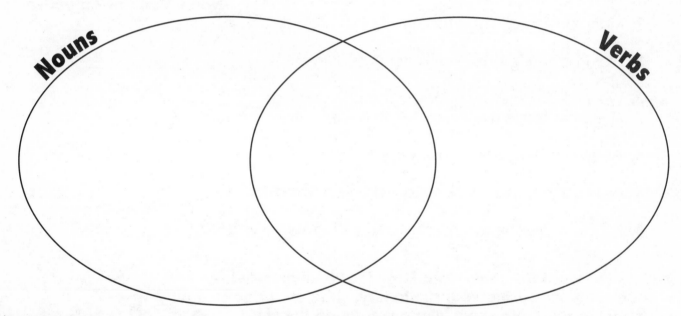

Nouns   **Verbs**

▶ **Choose two words from the overlapping section of the diagram. Use a dictionary to find a noun definition and a verb definition for each word. Write two sentences for each word using each definition.**

1. Noun _____

_____

Verb _____

_____

2. Noun _____

_____

Verb _____

_____

Name _____ Date _____

Multiple Mania

➤ **Use the dictionary entry to answer the questions.**

---

block /blok/ **n.** 1. A piece of wood 2. A platform from which property is sold at auction 3. A football play 4. A mold on which items are shaped 5. A line of houses enclosed by streets **v.** 1. To keep from passing 2. To shut off from view

---

1. How many noun definitions are given for *block*? _____

2. How many verb definitions are given for *block*? _____

➤ **Write the correct definition of *block* on each line.**

3. Thick trees *block* the sun from the forest floor.

_____

4. Seth lives on the same *block* as I do.

_____

➤ **Write a sentence using the following definitions of *block*.**

5. The second noun definition

_____

6. The first verb definition

_____

➤ **Use a dictionary to complete the entry for the word *part*.**

7. part /part/

   n. 1. _____

      2. _____

      3. _____

   v. 1. _____

      2. _____

Try This! Write one sentence using the word *part* three times with three different meanings.

Reading Between the Lines

▶ **Shade in the circle beside the dictionary entry that best defines the underlined word in the sentence.**

1. Neil pulled the <u>bark</u> away from the tree and exposed the wood underneath.
   ○ bark 1. Outer covering of a tree trunk
   ○ bark 2. Sound a dog makes

2. Tyrone needed to <u>wind</u> his watch because it was not keeping time correctly.
   ○ wind 1. Movement of air
   ○ wind 2. To tighten or turn

Tick Tick Tick
Tick Tick Tick

3. You should exercise regularly to keep your <u>organs</u> healthy and strong.
   ○ organs 1. Musical instruments
   ○ organs 2. Parts of a human or animal

4. Juan walked along the <u>bank</u> of the river looking for toads.
   ○ bank 1. A place to keep money
   ○ bank 2. The side of a river

5. The trapeze artist will <u>draw</u> a large crowd to her show this Saturday night.
   ○ draw 1. Attract
   ○ draw 2. To sketch or illustrate

▶ **Write a sentence for each definition you did not choose as the answer above.**

1. _____
   _____

2. _____
   _____

3. _____
   _____

4. _____
   _____

5. _____
   _____

What Are Encyclopedias?

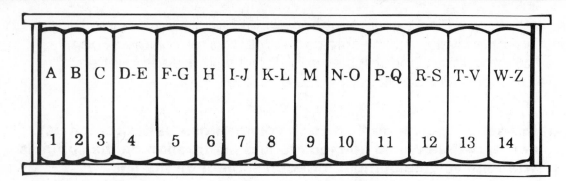

Encyclopedias are classified in the 000 section of the Dewey Decimal Classification® system under Generalities. However, they are usually kept in a special section of the library which is set aside for reference books, such as encyclopedias, dictionaries, atlases, and almanacs.

When you are assigned a topic for a report or project, a good place to start looking for information is in an encyclopedia. An encyclopedia will give you a general overview of the topic. However, you will usually want to find additional information from other sources that explore the topic more in-depth. The encyclopedia will give you information about people, places, and things, and answer the questions *who?*, *where?*, *when?*, and *how?*. But an encyclopedia usually does not answer the question *why?* or discuss both sides of a controversial subject in depth.

There are several things you should know about an encyclopedia so that you can use it easily and quickly.

You should know ...

- how the encyclopedia is arranged.
- how to use the index or the cross references.
- how to choose a good keyword when you are looking for a subject.
- how to use the guide words at the top of every page.
- how to read and use the illustrations, such as pictures, charts, graphs, maps, diagrams, etc.

Encyclopedias are usually arranged alphabetically on bookshelves. Usually you can turn directly to the volume containing the letter of the alphabet with which your subject begins. For example, if you want an article about Spain, you can turn directly to the Volume S and look for the subject alphabetically. You will notice that large subjects are divided into parts, such as climate, population, industries, interesting sites, and more. These subtopic headings may be in bold-face type.

Where Would You Look?

An encyclopedia is filled with information about people, places, and things. A set of encyclopedias contains many books, or volumes. Each volume has information about subjects that start with the same letter. They are arranged alphabetically on the bookshelf.

➤ **Look at this set of encyclopedias. Each volume has a letter (or letters) and a number. Where would you look to find information on the subjects below? Write the volume number for each subject on the line.**

A	B	C	D-E	F-G	H	I-J	K-L	M	N-O	P-Q	R-S	T-V	W-Z
1	2	3	4	5	6	7	8	9	10	11	12	13	14

1. dolphins _____

2. pheasants _____

3. rubber _____

4. Massachusetts _____

5. ships _____

6. deltoids _____

7. Egypt _____

8. anatomy _____

9. libraries _____

10. winds _____

11. Washington, D.C. _____

12. computers _____

13. wheat _____

14. koalas _____

15. paper _____

16. dolls _____

17. Ice Age _____

18. diamonds _____

19. x-rays _____

20. dachshunds _____

How many volumes does this set of encyclopedias have? _____

Name _____ Date _____

A Wealth of Information

Encyclopedias are a good place to look for information about a subject. If you're doing a report on water, the Great Depression, Sacagawea, or Nagasaki, you are sure to find some helpful and useful information in an encyclopedia.

When using an encyclopedia to learn about a certain person, use the first letter of his or her last name to direct you to the correct volume to use. For example, if you wanted to learn about Vincent Van Gogh, you would look for the volume that contains subjects that start with the letter *V*.

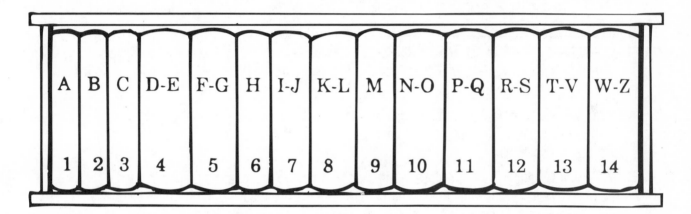

A	B	C	D-E	F-G	H	I-J	K-L	M	N-O	P-Q	R-S	T-V	W-Z
1	2	3	4	5	6	7	8	9	10	11	12	13	14

➤ **Look at the set of encyclopedias. Next to each subject below, write the volume number for the encyclopedia you would use.**

1. the Pacific Ocean _____

2. Robert E. Lee _____

3. Afghanistan _____

4. money _____

5. F. Scott Fitzgerald _____

6. eagles _____

7. Greg Norman _____

8. cotton _____

9. plutonium _____

10. blizzards _____

11. Johann Sebastian Bach _____

12. pharmacies _____

13. Bulgaria _____

14. black hole _____

15. War of 1812 _____

16. Catherine the Great _____

17. Hernando Cortes _____

18. photosynthesis _____

19. Charles Schultz _____

20. Jacques Cousteau _____

Tricky Situation

When a topic has more than one word, it may be difficult to choose the correct keyword to look for in the encyclopedia. Here are a few general rules:

1. You will find information about a person under his or her last name. Abraham Lincoln would be found under *L* for Lincoln.

2. If a person has a title, you will find information about him or her under the last part of his or her name. Queen Elizabeth would be found under *E* for Elizabeth. President Johnson would be found under *J* for Johnson.

3. If a subject has two or more parts, you will usually find it under the first part. North America would be found under *N* for North. Pacific Ocean would be found under *P* for Pacific. Space travel would be found under *S* for Space.

4. You will not find words or subjects under their abbreviations. Look for them as if they were spelled out. St. Paul (city) would be found under *Sa* for Saint Paul.

5. You will usually find a subject under the more specific topic name. For example, look for Baseball under *B* for Baseball, not *S* for Sports. However, if you are not sure which word to look under, the index or cross references will help you. Also note the additional topics listed under the main topics in the index or the cross references.

Which Word is Key?

➤ **Look at the topics below. Circle the word or words in each topic that you think would lead you to the encyclopedia volume that would have the information you need. Write the letter of the volume you would use on the line.**

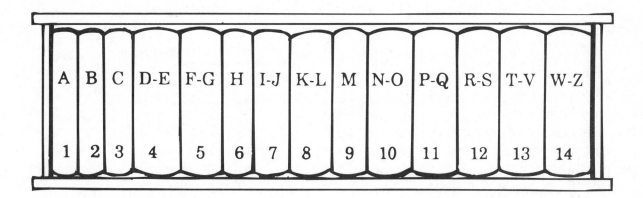

A	B	C	D-E	F-G	H	I-J	K-L	M	N-O	P-Q	R-S	T-V	W-Z
1	2	3	4	5	6	7	8	9	10	11	12	13	14

1. The use of atomic energy _____

2. The history of the Democratic party _____

3. The birthplace of President James Madison _____

4. The members of the North Atlantic Treaty Organization _____

5. The climate of Australia _____

6. The size of the Atlantic Ocean _____

7. The population of Madison, Wisconsin _____

8. The birthday of Queen Elizabeth II of Great Britain _____

9. The nationality of Sir Isaac Newton _____

10. The uses of guided missiles _____

11. The location of the Appalachian Mountains _____

12. The rules for playing ice hockey _____

13. The history of the radio _____

14. The number of post offices in the United States _____

15. President William Taft's middle name _____

Cross References

Sometimes you cannot get all the information you need on a topic from one encyclopedia article. If you need more information for your report, look at the very end of the encyclopedia article. Here you will find other places to search for information. These places are called **cross-references**. They are the topics under which you can find related information about your topic. Let's say you found information about the postal service under postal service. Now look at the cross-reference.

Postal Service—see also airmail; pony express; stamps

The *see also* references show you where to look to see additional information on your topic. These references are written in alphabetical order so they are easy to use. If you find additional information in a second encyclopedia article, check the end of that article, as well. It may give you other articles to check. Most articles have *see also* references. These are very valuable and can make your search for information easier and a lot more fun.

▶ **Find two topics in an encyclopedia that have *see also* references. Write the topics below and the *see also* references.**

Topic	*See also* references
1. _____	_____
	_____
2. _____	_____
	_____

Name _____ Date _____

See Also...

➤ **Look at the *see also* reference below. Write the *see also* reference that will help you find information for each topic.**

> Transportation—see also airplanes; automobiles; highways; railroads; ships; and travel

1. vacation travel _____

2. early sailing vessels _____

3. the Wright brothers' first plane _____

4. the invention of the automobile _____

5. mail planes _____

6. taking a cross-country trip _____

7. learning how to captain a boat _____

8. antique boats _____

9. racing cars _____

10. learning to fly _____

11. sailing around the world _____

12. railroad safety _____

Where in the World?

Encyclopedias are a good source of general information. When taking notes from an encyclopedia (or any other source), only write down key words and phrases. Do not copy sentences word-for-word from the encyclopedia. After you are finished taking notes, you can go back and create sentences of your own using the facts you have written down. This makes your report your own and helps you understand the material more than if you copy sentences exactly as you find them in an encyclopedia.

▶ **Choose a country to research in an encyclopedia. Find the following information:**

1. Location _____

2. Its size in square miles or kilometers _____

3. Language(s) spoken _____

4. Holidays _____

5. Climate _____

6. Economy _____

_____

7. Leaders in recent history _____

On a separate sheet of paper, write a short report about the country you chose. Include all of the information from above.

Reference Material Information

_____

Encyclopedia

_____   _____

Volume   Page

Snooping Around

Encyclopedias are a good place to look for information about a famous person. You can learn about a figure from history, such as Nostradamus, or someone a little more contemporary, such as Robert Redford. As with any other subject, only write down key words and phrases when taking notes for a report. Don't copy someone else's words—that is called plagiarism!

➤ Choose a person that you would like to learn more about. Look him or her up in an encyclopedia. Find the following information:

1. Where and when he/she was born _____

   _____

2. Where he/she grew up _____

   _____

3. Why he/she is famous _____

   _____

   _____

4. Any other important information _____

   _____

   _____

On a separate sheet of paper, write a short report about the person you chose. Include all of the information from above.

Reference Material Information

_____

Encyclopedia

_____   _____

Volume   Page

U.S. States and Presidents

➤ **Use encyclopedias to answer the questions below.**

Across
4. What is the main agricultural product in Kansas?
5. What is the state bird of Lincoln's birthplace?
6. What river is near President Franklin Roosevelt's birthplace?
7. Thomas Jefferson was born in what state?
8. What president followed Theodore Roosevelt into the White House?
9. What state became a state when Theodore Roosevelt was in office?
10. What is the smallest state in the United States?

Down
1. Andrew Jackson died in what city?
2. What is the capital of the state where Abraham Lincoln was born?
3. The president who followed Lincoln into the White House was born in what city?

Name _____ Date _____

Web of Information

Use an encyclopedia to find information about the following subject:

_____

▶ **Using the web below, record important information about your subject. You may add more circles if needed.**

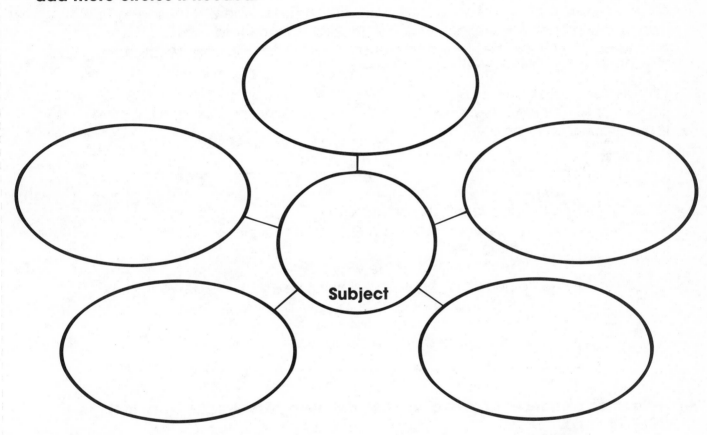

Subject

On a separate sheet of paper, write a short report about your subject. Include your information from above.

Reference Material Information

_____

Encyclopedia

_____ _____

Volume   Page

Name _____ Date _____

What's Another Word For...?

When you need to find a synonym for a word, open up your **thesaurus**. A thesaurus is a book of synonyms that you can use to help spice up your writing.

Sometimes the same word keeps popping up in your head. You want to describe someone as being *nice*, but you don't want to keep using the word *nice*. You know there is a different word that would have the same effect. This is where a thesaurus can come in handy. For example, if you looked up the word *nice* in a thesaurus, you might see the words *friendly*, *kind*, *pleasant*, and *amiable*. These are all synonyms for the word *nice*.

Sometimes words can be used in different ways to mean different things. For example, the word *rest* can be used as a noun and as a verb. Look at the thesaurus entry below.

---

rest
1. nap, sleep, snooze, doze
   My brother needed a **rest** after playing soccer.
2. remainder
   I'll walk the **rest** of the way home.
3. to sleep, take a break, slow down, relax, lie down
   I need to **rest** after that long walk.
4. to stand, prop, lean, put
   Rest the broom against the wall.

► **Write three sentences of your own using the word *rest*. Use the word in three different ways.**

1. _____

2. _____

3. _____

Use the activity below with your students to reinforce the importance of using a thesaurus.

Write the following sentence on the whiteboard or overhead:
The pretty diamond ring was displayed in the jewelry store window.

Ask your students if the word *pretty* is a good descriptive word to use for a diamond ring. Ask them what other choices might be more exact in describing a diamond.

Show your students a thesaurus and explain how it is used (if it is new to your students). Tell them that a thesaurus usually shows the following information:
- the parts of speech of a word
- the word's meaning or phrase
- the use of a word in a sample sentence or phrase
- synonyms for a word
- antonyms for a word

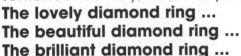

Have your students look up *pretty* in a thesaurus. Ask them which of the following synonyms for *pretty* would make sense in the sentence: comely, fair, lovely, beautiful, pleasing, or brilliant.
The lovely diamond ring ...
The beautiful diamond ring ...
The brilliant diamond ring ...
All three of these would be acceptable, but the word brilliant is more exact in describing a diamond. The word ugly is given as the antonym.

Write the following words on index cards and distribute them to students:

angry	clear	fat	important	perfect	thin
big	create	finish	jump	pull	try
bold	decide	funny	laugh	quick	unite
bring	easy	gather	look	same	upset
careful	effect	give	many	see	warning
change	examine	great	new	sharp	while
clean	fake	happy	nice	source	wish

Have each student use a thesaurus to find a word, its meaning, its synonyms, and its antonyms. Have them write sentences using the original word. Then, have them rewrite the sentence using one of the word's synonyms.

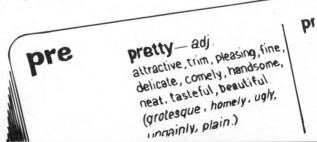

pre | pr

pretty— *adj.*
attractive, trim, pleasing, fine, delicate, comely, handsome, neat, tasteful, beautiful. (grotesque, homely, ugly, ungainly, plain.)

The 'Fraidy Brontosaurus

➤ **Use a thesaurus to find synonyms for each word under a line.**

Once upon a time there was a _____ brontosaurus who lived in a cave with his _____ wife.
<u>large</u> ... <u>sweet</u>

"Please, dear," Bernice said, "_____ down to the forest and _____ up some
<u>walk</u> ... <u>snatch</u>
shrubs for dinner. But be careful not to go near the mouse house. Remember what
happened the last time you ran into the mouse family?"

Bobby Brontosaurus walked _____ down to the forest. When he reached the
<u>slowly</u>
mouse house, he was overcome with _____. He had to _____ inside the hole.
<u>interest</u> ... <u>look</u>
He saw the mice finishing their _____ of hot tea and cheese.
<u>meal</u>

"Oh, here we go again," said Mrs. Mouse. "I thought we scared him off for good last
time. Well, you know what this means," she _____.
<u>exhaled</u>

The mice came _____ out of their little house and scared Bobby silly. They ran
<u>running</u>
up over his back and down his tail. Their little feet tickled his spine as they _____
<u>ran</u>
across him. Bobby was _____ with fear and laughter all at once. He _____ in
<u>filled</u> ... <u>dropped</u>
the grass and bushes, rolling with laughter.

What a _____! Four cute _____ mice in scarves, goggles, and helmets with
<u>scene</u> ... <u>little</u>
ear flaps scaring the _____ creature in the forest. Despite Bobby's _____ size,
<u>largest</u> ... <u>large</u>
he was _____ of anything that moved below him.
<u>scared</u>

The mouse family _____ with laughter. Bobby managed to _____ to his feet
<u>wailed</u> ... <u>get</u>
and run off to his wife. In all the _____, he had forgotten about getting their dinner
<u>uproar</u>
until he reached the cave. Bernice opened the door and smiled with _____.
<u>gladness</u>

"Oh, my," she said, "You have outdone yourself."

She reached behind him and _____ shrubs and branches off his back.
<u>took</u>

"I've never seen you _____ our dinner home on your back before, but any way
<u>carry</u>
you bring it home is fine with me," she said and gave him a big, _____ kiss right on
<u>wet</u>
his cheek.

Name _____ Date _____

What Is an Almanac?

An almanac is a reference material just like a dictionary, encyclopedia, and thesaurus. It is a collection of information and facts for people of all different walks of life. In an almanac, you might find information on the tides, weather forecasts, current events, calendars, presidents, religions, health, historical anniversaries, and so much more.

Almanacs are updated and changed every year to reflect current events. Since the late 1700s, farmers have been using almanacs to schedule the planting of their crops, and people living near oceans have found the tide tables helpful. Almanacs can also include tables and charts about the planets, eclipses, longitude, and latitude that might be helpful to sailors on ships.

Today, almanacs contain a larger variety of facts than years ago. They can include recipes, information on gardening, animals, wedding traditions, pets, consumer trends, nature, and more. There are also many online almanacs that contain loads of fun facts, tips, stories, this day in history information, questions of the day, and local forecasts.

► **Check out these almanac websites for information on, well, almost anything. While you're there, write down two interesting facts that you learn from each website. Share your facts with a classmate.**

www.almanac.com

_____

_____

www.worldalmanacforkids.com

_____

_____

www.worldalmanac.com

_____

_____

www.farmersalmanac.com

_____

_____

Name _____ Date _____

Facts Online

Almanacs can be found in most school libraries. You will find them in the reference section, along with the dictionaries and encyclopedias. If your library has Internet service, you also have access to online almanacs. The online versions of almanacs are usually updated daily with weather forecasts, horoscopes, questions of the day, tips of the day, and much more. Online almanacs contain a wealth of interesting, useful information that is worth browsing through. And hey, you might just learn something!

➡ **Go to the websites below. Use the websites to answer the questions.**

World Almanac For Kids at www.worldalmanacforkids.com

1. What is the name of the amusement park in Denmark? _____

2. What is the definition of ecosystem? _____
_____

3. What was Gerald R. Ford's given name at birth? _____
Why was it changed? _____

4. Who invented the helicopter? _____
What year was it invented? _____

5. What famous people do you share a birthday with? _____

The Farmers Almanac at www.farmersalmanac.com

1. What is the gardening tip of the day? _____

2. What dates will there be a full moon this year? _____

The Old Farmer's Almanac at www.almanac.com

1. What happened on this day in history? _____

2. Find a recipe for something that sounds good to you. Write the name of it on the line. _____

3. What is happening this month with the moon and stars? _____
_____

Name _____ Date _____

What Is an Atlas?

An **atlas** is a reference book. It is a book filled with maps of places that span the globe. Atlases can also contain charts and tables, too. You can learn about cities, towns, roads, countries, rivers, and mountains in an atlas.

You will find two types of maps in an atlas. The first is a physical map which shows the physical features of a country, such as rivers, deserts, mountains, plains, and lakes. The second type of map is a political map. A political map shows boundaries and important cities. An atlas also has an index in the back to help you locate a map you are looking for.

► **Use an atlas to answer the questions below.**

1. On what page can you find the state in which you live? _____

2. On what page can you find a physical map of New Zealand? _____

3. On what page can you find a political map of Asia? _____

4. List three countries that you can find on a political map of Europe.

   _____

5. On what page can you find a political map of France? _____

6. What is the capital city of France? _____

7. Find a physical map of the United States. What is the longest river? _____

8. Where is it located? _____

9. What is the name of your atlas? _____

► **Use an atlas and write three questions of your own. Trade with a classmate and answer each other's questions.**

1. _____

   Answer: _____

2. _____

   Answer: _____

3. _____

   Answer: _____

Name _____ Date _____

Finding Your Way Around

You are going on vacation this summer and you promised your dad that you would learn how to read a map. In most atlases, you will see letters along the sides of a map and numbers along the top and bottom of a map. These help you find cities. For example, Quincy can be found at H1 on the map below.

➡ **Look at the map below. Notice the letters and numbers on the outside of the map. Write the location of each city below.**

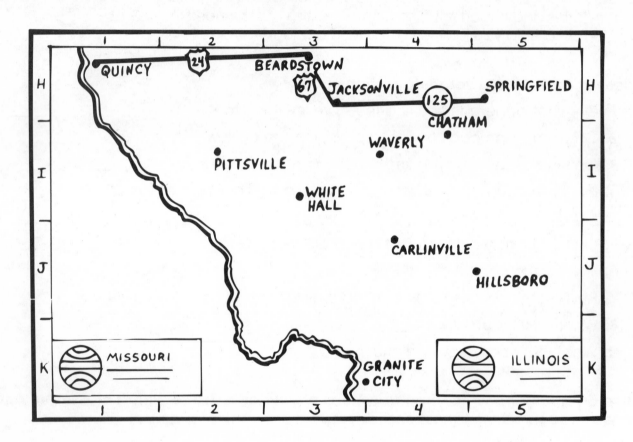

Jacksonville _____   Hillsboro _____

Beardstown _____   Pittsville _____

White Hall _____   Chatham _____

Carlinville _____   Granite City _____

Waverly _____

Magazines

Most libraries have a supply of magazines for students to read and use. There will be times when you will need information from a magazine. There are many different types of magazines, and every magazine is different. Sometimes you can tell what subjects you will find in a magazine by reading its title. You can also look through the table of contents to get more information about what's inside.

Magazines contain useful information on a variety of topics. The information you will find in a magazine is up-to-date. Sometimes you will be able to find the most recent information on a subject in a magazine. Magazines are a kind of **periodical**. They are printed periodically—some are printed once a month, others are printed every few months. This is why the information inside is so current.

The table of contents in a magazine is a good place to look to see exactly what is included in the magazine. Just like in a book, the table of contents can be found at the beginning of a magazine. You can use it to see the article titles, the authors, and the page numbers on which the articles start.

Name _____   Date _____

The Magazine Table of Contents

The table of contents can show you where to find articles in a magazine. Knowing where to find the information you need will help your research go faster and smoother.

▶ **Look at the table of contents below. Answer the questions that follow.**

Let's Get Cooking

**Learning to Cook:
A Guide for Kids**
by James Stove 14

Baking Cookies
by Cookie Crumble 24

Buying the Right Ingredients
by James Checklist 29

Using Flour in Your Recipes
by Wendy Wheat 31

Baking Special Holiday Treats
by Holly J. Holiday 37

Baking Cakes
by Mark Marble 46

Nutrition and Baking
by Vera Vitamins 51

How to Cook Vegetables
by Barbara Broccoli 63

Buying a Cook Book
by Mia Money 73

I. To learn about nutrition and baking, which article should you turn to?

_____

2. If you are baking a chocolate cake, which article should you use?

_____

3. Which article should you read if you want to know how to stock your cupboards with the baking essentials? _____

4. Which article should you read if you want to learn how to make baklava, a Greek favorite during the holidays? _____

5. Which article should you read if you are a young, beginning cook?

_____

6. If you wanted to bake sugar cookies, which article should you read?

_____

7. If you wanted to learn how to cook asparagus, which article should you read?

_____

Which Magazine Should I Choose?

➤ **Look at the magazine titles below. Answer the questions using one of the titles.**

Shark and Sea Life Magazine   Dog Magazine

Whales   Animals of the Wild

Science Magazine for Kids   Rhyme Time Magazine

American History for Kids   Putting on a Play

Weather Magazine   Insect Digest

I. You are writing a report about clouds. Which magazine should you use?
_____

2. You have to find information on jellyfish. Which magazine should you use?
_____

3. You are giving a presentation on the Westward Movement. Which magazine will have useful information for you?_____

4. You want to sketch a picture of a chimpanzee. Which magazine could you use for a reference?_____

5. You are in charge of building the backdrop for your class play. Which magazine could help you get started?_____

6. You're wondering how a doorbell works. Which magazine might have an article on doorbells?_____

7. In the woods yesterday you caught a large, six-legged creature that flies. You're fascinated by it because you've never seen anything like it. Which magazine might help you identify it?_____

8. Your English assignment is to write a haiku. You have no idea what this is. Which magazine should you look in? _____

9. Your new puppy has chewed your favorite pair of shoes and is digging in the backyard. She is your responsibility and your dad is getting upset at you and the dog. Which magazine might have some training tips?

_____

10. You heard a news story about whales washing up on shore and having to be rescued. You're intrigued and want to learn more about whale migration. Which magazine should you pick up?_____

Running References

You have learned about the reference materials that are available in your library—dictionaries, encyclopedias, thesauruses, almanacs, and atlases. Each one can be used for a variety of reasons.

▶ **Cut out the faucets and drops of water below. Figure out where you would look to find the information on each drop (which reference material would you use?). On a separate sheet of paper, glue the drops under the faucets of the reference material you would use.**

Encyclopedia	Dictionary	Atlas	Almanac	Thesaurus

correct spelling of *assimilation*	synonyms for the word *loud*	physical features of India	the life of King Tut	the weather in Nairobi
antonym for the word *steady*	meaning of the word *faint*	the location of Venice on a map	general information on the Seven Wonders of the World	parts of speech of the word *smile*
the population of Green Bay, Wisconsin	another word for *loyal*	highways that run through Utah	inventor of the toaster	chief products of China

Name _____ Date _____

100–199 Philosophy & Psychology

Do you like to think about things? Are there some things that you just wonder about all the time? If so, this second section of the nonfiction books might be your favorite. It is the Philosophy and Psychology section. This section contains books about the mind and feelings. Look at the sub-sections of this section below.

100 Philosophy & Psychology

100 Metaphysics

120 Epistemology, Causation, Humankind

130 Paranormal Phenomena & Arts

140 Specific Philosophical Viewpoints

150 Psychology

160 Logic

170 Ethics

180 Ancient, Medieval, Oriental

190 Modern Western Philosophy

▶ **Choose one of the activities below to familiarize yourself with this section of the library.**

How Did You Know?—Read a book on ESP or abnormally good brain power. Write a report on what you learn.

I Feel So ...—Choose an emotion, such as happ[y], excitement, fear, etc. Find a book on this emoti[on]. Write a report on what you learn.

A Great Friendship—Find a book about frien[ds]hip. Think of someone in your life who has been [a] [g]ood friend to you. Write about your experiences [tog]ether and what makes this person such a good fr[ie]nd.

x

x

x

Name _____ Date _____

200–299 Religion & Mythology

The 200–299 section of the nonfiction books contains books on religion and mythology. You can read about religious celebrations around the world and characters in Greek mythology. Look at the sub-sections of this section below.

200 Religion & Mythology

210 Natural Religion

220 Bible

230 Christian Theology

240 Christian Moral & Devotional

250 Local Church & Religious Orders

260 Social & Ecclesiastical Theology

270 History & Geography of Church

280 Christian Denomination & Sects

290 Other & Comparative Religions

▶ **Choose one of the activities below to familiarize yourself with this section of the library.**

So That Explains It!—Find a mythology book that explains events in the world, such as why the sky is blue or why dogs have tails. Now write your own myth explaining something different.

Let's Celebrate—Learn about a religious celebration or festival that you don't know a lot about. Create a symbol of this celebration and present it to your class.

It's All Greek To Me—Read about a god/goddess in Greek mythology, such as Zeus, Aphrodite, or Atlas. Write a paper describing what this god or goddess is known for.

Name _____ Date _____

300–399 Social Sciences

The Social Sciences section of the library has the call numbers 300–399. It contains books on the environment, education, government, legends, fairy tales, and folktales. Look at the sub-sections below.

300 Social Sciences

310 Statistics

320 Political Science

330 Economics

340 Law

350 Public Administration & Military Science

360 Social Pathology & Services

370 Education

380 Commerce, Communication & Transportation

390 Customs & Folklore

▶ **Choose one of the activities below to familiarize yourself with this section of the library.**

Which Version Is It?—Find a fairy tale that has more than one version, such as Cinderella. Read two or more versions and compare and contrast them using a Venn diagram.

Help Mother Earth—Learn about ways that we can all help keep our planet clean. Give a presentation to your classmates telling them what they can do to help. Create visual aids, such as graphs, posters, or illustrations that demonstrate the importance of everyone helping, no matter how small. Use the visual aids during your presentation to persuade your classmates into action.

The Three Rs—Recycle! Reduce! Reuse! Read a book about recycling and cleaning up after ourselves. Create signs to put up around your school that stress the importance of recycling, reducing, and reusing.

Name _____ Date _____

400–499 Language

You will find the language section of the library in the 400-499 area. This section contains books on almost any language that you would want to learn about. If you are traveling to another country and want to learn some new words to use while you are there, look in this section. Or if you just want to impress your parents by saying, "Thank you!" in Italian, this section is for you.

400 Language

410 Linguistics

420 English & Anglo-Saxon Languages

430 German

440 French—Romance Languages

450 Italian, Romanian, & Rhaeto-Romantic Languages

460 Spanish & Portuguese Languages

470 Latin

480 Greek

490 Other Languages

 Choose one of the activities below to familiarize yourself with this section of the library.

Which Way to the Bathroom?—Choose a language that you would like to learn more about. Make a list of words in this language that you want to learn and practice saying them with a friend.

Where Is It Spoken?—Choose a language and do some research to find out where it is spoken around the world. On a map of the world, color the areas where the language is spoken.

Written Languages—Some written languages use picture-like symbols instead of letters, such as Chinese and Japanese. Do some research on one of these languages and learn some symbols to use. Practice using them with a friend.

0-7424-1954-1 *Complete Library Skills*

500–599 Science

The science section of the nonfiction books occupies the 500-599 area of the library. This section contains books on chemistry, astronomy, math, animals, dinosaurs, and so much more. Look at the sub-sections of the Science section below.

500 Science

510 Mathematics

520 Astronomy & Allied Sciences

530 Physics

540 Chemistry & Allied Sciences

550 Sciences of Earth & Other Worlds

560 Paleontology

570 Life Sciences

580 Botanical Sciences

590 Zoological Sciences

▶ **Choose one of the activities below to familiarize yourself with this section of the library.**

Shaking Like a Leaf—Research different types of trees and their leaves. Draw and label leaves for each type of tree you learn about.

Fruitful Trees—Make a list of fruit that grows on trees. Include the climate that each type of tree grows in.

Far, Far Away—Do some research on a planet. Learn about the planet's size, distance from Earth and the sun, temperature, and any other information that interests you. Write a report describing this planet in-depth.

600–699 Useful Arts

The useful arts section of the library will teach you what you need to know about medicine, inventions, gardening, and more. This section also contains how-to books for many different projects, such as carpentry, model building, and making things with leather. The useful arts section can be found in the area of the library numbered 600–699.

600 Useful Arts

610 Medical Sciences

620 Engineering & Allied Operations

630 Agricultural & Related Technologies

640 Domestic Arts & Sciences

650 Managerial & Business Services

660 Chemical & Related Technologies

670 Manufacturers

680 Miscellaneous Manufacturers

690 Buildings

 Choose one of the activities below to familiarize yourself with this section of the library.

Hello, Doctor—Read about a famous person in the medical field. It could be a doctor, nurse, researcher—anyone who has made an impact on medicine. Write a report about this person's accomplishments and impact on the medical field.

Do You Have a Green Thumb?—Do some research on plants and flowers that can grow in your area of the country. Make a list of things you could plant in your yard at home.

Who Invented That?—Find a book on inventions. Write a paragraph or two on an inventor or invention that fascinates you. Make sure you include how the invention was created or why it was needed.

Name _____ Date _____

700–799 Fine Arts

The fine arts section of the library can be found in the 700-799 area. This section contains books on art, music, sports, and hobbies.

700 Fine Arts

710 Civic & Landscape Art

720 Architecture

730 Plastic Arts—Sculpture

740 Drawing, Decorative, & Minor Arts

750 Painting & Paintings

760 Graphic Arts—Prints

770 Photography & Photographs

780 Music

790 Recreational & Performing Arts

 Choose one of the activities below to familiarize yourself with this section of the library.

What a Building!—Think of a building that fascinates you, such as the Empire State Building or the Seattle Space Needle. Learn about this building and write a short report on the architect who designed it and the details of this building. Illustrate a picture of the building to accompany your report.

It's Magnificent!—Use a book on art to find a painting that interests you. Find out who the artist is and learn more about him or her. Illustrate the painting and write a short biography of the artist.

Draw It!—Use a book on drawing to learn how to draw something new.

800–899 Literature

The literature section of the library contains American and foreign literature, as well as plays, poems, and essays. This section can be found in the 800–899 area of the library. You can find a collection of favorite poems, Shakespeare plays, and foreign poetry here. Look at the sub-sections below.

800 Languages

810 American Literature in English

820 English & Anglo-Saxon Literature

830 German Literature

840 French Literature

850 Italian, Romanian, & Rhaeto-Romantic Literatures

860 Spanish & Portuguese Literatures

870 Latin Literature

880 Greek Literature

890 Literature of Other Languages

 Choose one of the activities below to familiarize yourself with this section of the library.

Music to My Ears—Read about a famous poet. Write a short biography of his or her life. Be sure to include titles of the poems he or she is famous for.

Play It—Choose a play to read. Describe the elements of the play, such as the characters, setting, problems, and solutions. Did you like this play? Why or why not?

My Favorite—Read a book of poetry. Choose a poem that you really like. Copy it onto a piece of paper and illustrate it. Write a sentence or two about why you chose this poem as one of your favorites.

Name _____ Date _____

900–999 Geography & History

To learn all about the continents and countries of the world, find the geography and history section of the library. This section also contains biographies about people of importance. This is the last section of the nonfiction books and can be found in the 900–999 area.

900 Geography & History

910 Geography—Travel

920 Biography, Genealogy, & Insigna

930 History of the Ancient World

940 History of Europe

950 History of Asia

960 History of Africa

970 History of North America

980 History of South America

990 History of Other Parts of the World

 Choose one of the activities below to familiarize yourself with this section of the library.

Web of Information—Read about a famous person who interests you. Create a web of information about this person's life, starting with his or her name in the center circle.

Animal Planet—Choose a country to read about. Make a list of the animals that inhabit this country. State the factors that help these animals survive in this country (climate, diet, homes). Illustrate a few of these animals.

Where in the World?—Choose a country that you would like to visit someday. Read about the holidays they celebrate, the clothes they wear, the food they eat, what they do for fun, etc. Compare and contrast this country to the country in which you live using a Venn diagram.

Divide your class into small groups of two or three students. Reproduce the wheel below so that each group has a wheel. Use a paper clip to create a spinner that can be inserted through the middle spot on the wheel.

Have your students take turns spinning the Wheel of Dewey. For the title that they land on, they must be able to name the section of the library where they can find it. If they are right, they get a point. If they are wrong, they do not get a point. Play until all sections of the library have been identified for each title. The player with the most points wins.

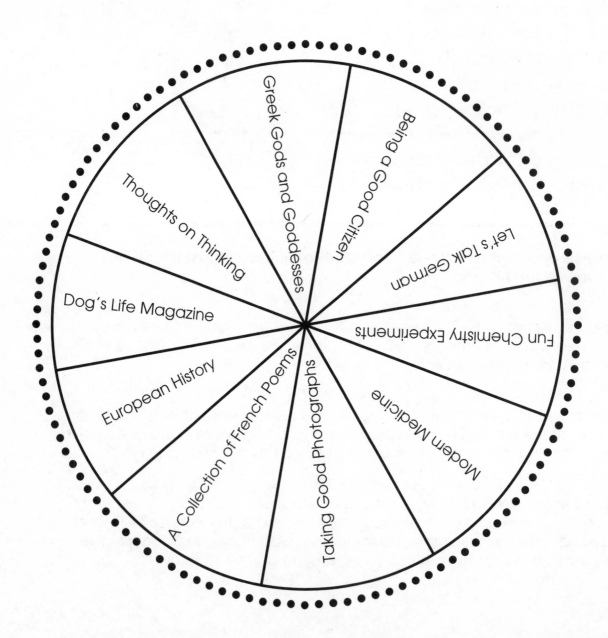

Use the following activities to reinforce and practice the ten nonfiction sections of the library.

Picture It!
Using a variety of magazines that you have collected (or your students have donated), have students find a picture that they can assign to one of the ten sections of the library. For example, a picture of a dolphin would belong in the 599 section of the nonfiction books (mammals). The student will cut out the picture and glue it to a large piece of paper ($11\frac{1}{2}$ x 18 inches) and label it with the correct section number and subject. You can either assign a number of pictures that students must find and label, assign a certain section to each student with more than one student having the same section, or have students find one or two pictures for each section of the nonfiction books.

What a Pair!
Assign a hundreds section to each student. Using the library, students must find at least four titles within the section they are given. They will write down each title on a small, square piece of paper (write only the title, not the call number). When they have finished writing their titles, they will turn them in to you and you will combine all book titles in a coffee can, bag, hat, or some other object that kids can reach into. When everyone has finished, each student will randomly pick four or five book titles from the collection of titles (if they choose one of theirs, they should put it back). They must figure out which section of the library each title can be found in and match each title to a section card (below). Make enough copies of the cards below so that each student has multiple cards of each subject if needed. On a large piece of paper ($11\frac{1}{2}$ x 18 inches), they will glue each book title and section card next to each other so that they become a pair.

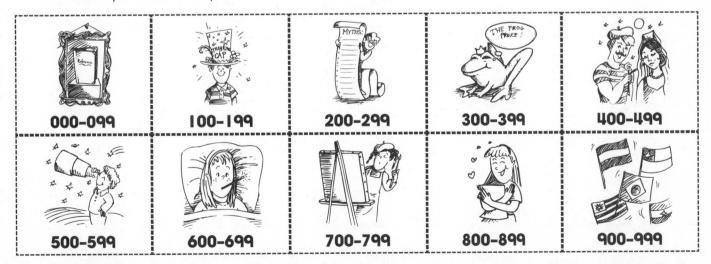

000–099	100–199	200–299	300–399	400–499
500–599	600–699	700–799	800–899	900–999

 0-7424-1954-1 *Complete Library Skills*

Fun with Dewey

Dewey Bingo!

Reproduce copies of the blank Dewey bingo board below. Have your students fill in each square with a random Dewey call number (such as 190, 320, or 570). When everyone has finished filling in their Dewey bingo boards, call off titles of nonfiction books. Using either a chart on the classroom wall or a cheat sheet on each desk that shows the different Dewey sections and the call numbers, your students will cover up the spaces on their boards for book titles that fit into the call numbers they have written on their boards. For example, if you called off the title *The Amazing Planets*, students would look for the call number 520. If they have 520 somewhere on their Dewey bingo boards, they would cover it up with a chip or marker (whatever you have supplied). The first person to cover a row going up, down, or diagonally wins!

D	E	W	E	Y
		FREE SPACE		

Genres of Literature

No matter what you're in the mood to read, you can always find a book that is just right in the library. You can find books that teach you things, make you laugh, tell you about a person's life, make you tap your foot to a rhythm, or explain something about the real world. There are many different genres, or types of books, from which to choose. You never have to leave the library empty-handed.

► **Look at the web below. It shows you some genres you will find in your library.**

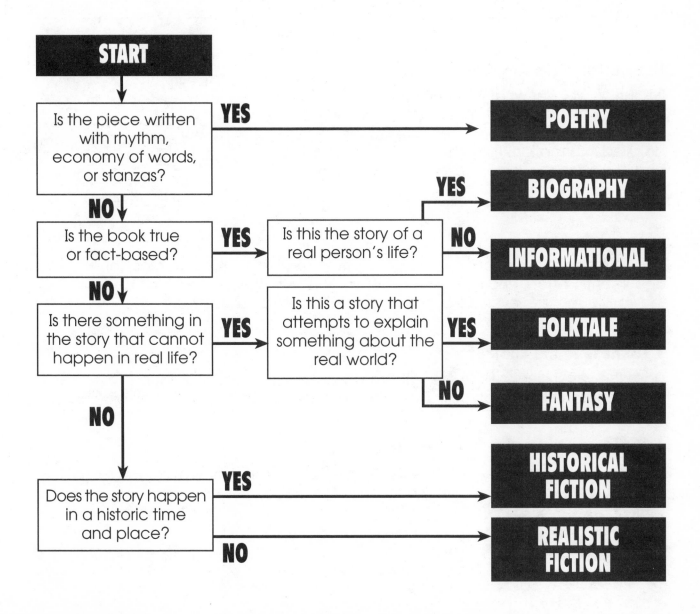

Biographies and Autobiographies

A biography is ...
- the history of a real person's life written by another person.
- a book that tells about the time and place in which the person lives or lived.
- a work that offers insight into the impact its subject had on people and events.
- a book that shows how the author feels about his or her subject.

An autobiography is ...
- the history of a person's life written by him- or herself.

How to Tell if It's Any Good

It is fun to wonder what it must have been like to live long ago. Biographies help satisfy that curiosity by making history and people come to life through detailed information. They also present role models and heroes to readers. An excellent biography should include:

• Accurate Facts

Is the information correct? Are the details from reliable sources such as court documents, letters, and interviews? Are all facts authentic to the date and time of the individual's life, even if the book has a fictional framework?

• Fairness to the Subject

Does the writer depict both strengths and weaknesses in the individual? Does the biographer avoid stereotypes? Does the author differentiate facts from opinions?

• Ways to Relate

Are the struggles and accomplishments of the subject vividly portrayed?

Hello, My Name Is...

A biography is a book about a person's life written by another person. It might include information such as when and where he or she was born, how many people were in his or her family, and the impact that he or she had on the world. Biographies include a lot of facts and true information and they are often used for reports or projects on famous people.

➤ **Choose a biography on a person you want to learn more about. Use the biography to take notes below. Use your notes to prepare a report that you will give on the person you have chosen. If possible, dress like your subject or use props when presenting to your class.**

My biography report is on _____.

Title of book _____

Author _____ Copyright date _____

Date of birth _____ Place of birth _____

What was this person's childhood like?

_____

_____

_____

What is this person known for?

_____

_____

Did he or she have to overcome obstacles/trouble in life?

☐ Yes ☐ No

If so, what? _____

If you could meet this person in real life, what would you like to ask him or her?

_____

_____

List two things you learned about this person.

_____

_____

Biography Call Numbers

You can read about someone's life in a biography. This is a book that is written by someone other than the subject of the book, but the author has done research so that he or she can write about the person. The call number of a biography is 921. After the call number you will see two letters—these two letters are the first two letters of the subject's last name (the person whom the book is about). Look at the example.

The Life of Ramona Peabody
by James Bernstein

921
Pe

➤ **Look at the biographies below. Write the call number on the line next to each biography.**

1. *Captain Hook—Life of a Pirate* by Edward Johnson   _____

2. *Sir Francis Drake—The Explorer* by James Mitchell   _____

3. *The Life of a President—Gerald R. Ford* by Don Bartell   _____

4. *The Life of First Lady Nancy Reagan* by Anne Ludlow   _____

5. *Walt Disney* by Albert Compton   _____

6. *Babe Ruth—Baseball's Hero* by Roger Dalton   _____

7. *Betsy Ross—Daughter of the American Revolution*
   by Caroline Carter   _____

8. *The Three Tenors* by Michael Marsdale   _____

9. *Frank Lloyd Wright* by Annie Zaschak   _____

10. *The Life of Crazy Horse* by Robert Mizner   _____

Autobiography Call Numbers

An autobiography is similar to a biography. It is a book about a person, but it is written by the person that it is about. Your autobiography can only be written by you.

Autobiographies are also similar to biographies because they follow the same rules for the call number. You will find them in the 921 section of your library next to biographies. The two letters that follow 921 are the first two letters of the last name of the subject of the book (also the author). Look at the example.

Dr. Seuss—My Life by Dr. Seuss

921
Se

➤ **Look at the autobiographies below. Write the call numbers for each book on the lines.**

1. *Daniel Boone—My Life* by Daniel Boone _____

2. *Jim Henson—The Muppets and Me* by Jim Henson _____

3. *Mickey Mantle—My Life in Baseball* by Mickey Mantle _____

4. *My Life as a Genius* by Albert Einstein _____

5. *My Life as President of the United States* by Theodore Roosevelt _____

6. *In the Spotlight* by Sammy Davis Jr. _____

7. *Keeping Score* by Mia Hamm _____

8. *Life with Abe* by Mary Todd Lincoln _____

9. *Liberace—The Music Man* by Liberace _____

10. *George Washington—My Life* by George Washington _____

➤ **Find two autobiographies in your library that interest you. Write the titles, authors, and call numbers below.**

Title	Author	Call Number
1. _____	_____	_____
2. _____	_____	_____

It Could Really Happen!

Have you ever read a story and thought, *This could really happen.*
This kind of story is called **Realistic Fiction**.

Realistic fiction ...

- is a story that could happen, even if events are extraordinary or even improbable.
- is a story set in current times, not in historical times.
- is a story with a setting that is believable and vivid because it is described well.
- is a story with well-developed characters that are described through words, actions, and thoughts.
- has action or plot development that really holds the reader's interest.
- is a story with characters and conflicts that are well-developed.
- offers the reader the opportunity to look at his or her own feelings and actions, as well as others' feelings and actions.
- demonstrates that people are in charge of their own lives and can bring about change through their own actions.
- demonstrates that all people share common experiences.

How to Tell if It's Any Good

Realistic fiction offers its readers company. When you read a realistic fiction book, you do not feel so alone because it shows you that other people have feelings and face problems just like you do. Realistic fiction helps you realize that you have the power to make changes, without needing a fairy godmother or some other magic to rescue you. An example of an excellent work of realistic fiction should include:

- **Realism**
  Is the story possible, though not necessarily probable? Do the characters seem like actual people that you could know? Is the setting realistic and easy to picture?

- **Purpose**
  Does the story help you understand your own problems, feelings, or relationships? Does the story help you understand that people are more alike than different?

- **Ways to Relate**
  Can you identify with the character's feelings? Does the story present problems that you or your friends might actually face?

In Touch with Reality

Realistic fiction is easy to read and understand because of its realism. Could this made-up story really happen? Can I picture myself or a friend in this character's shoes? If you answer yes to these questions about a book, then it is probably **realistic fiction**.

▶ **Choose a realistic fiction book from your library. Read the book and then fill out the note card below. When you are finished taking notes, write a short summary of the book using the information from your notes.**

Title _____ Author _____

What is the setting of the book? _____

Describe the main character in the story. _____

_____

Who is telling the story? (point of view) _____

What is the main character's problem? _____

_____

Do you identify with the main character? If so, how?

_____

_____

How did the main character solve his/her problem?

_____

_____

How would you have solved this problem?

_____

_____

What elements of this story are realistic?

_____

_____

Read *Alexander and the Terrible, Horrible, No Good, Very Bad Day* by Judith Viorst to your students. Have them fill out the organizers below about their own good and bad days, mimicking the story.

How my bad day started:

The middle of my bad day:

How my bad day ended:

 Bad Day

People who shared my bad day:

The worst part of this day:

How my good day started:

The middle of my good day:

How my good day ended:

 Good Day

People who shared my good day:

The best part of this day:

Name _____ Date _____

Historical Fiction

Do you like reading books that take you back to a different period in history? Books that help you travel back to a time in history are called **Historical Fiction**.

Historical fiction ...
- is a fictional story set during an important historical period.
- combines a realistic story with factual information.
- includes some characters who might be fictional, and others who might be real people who lived during that historical period.
- has real and fictional events mixed into the plot.
- is a reading opportunity to learn more about a specific historical period or event.
- brings history alive through the characters and the details of everyday life, historical events, and differences in attitudes and beliefs.

How to Tell if It's Any Good

Historical fiction allows you to experience an historical period through a fictional character. Historical fiction, like biographies, offers insight, role models, and intimate knowledge of the past. An example of an excellent work of historical fiction should include:

- **Accuracy**
  Are the facts and details authentic and accurate to the historical setting? Is the language of the period reflected in the story? Does the writing reflect what people knew and thought about at that time? Does the story accurately reflect the values and spirit of the time? Is the problem in the story realistic for that period?

- **Fairness to the Reader**
  Are you free to judge the mistakes of the past themselves? There should not be a strong point of view stated or implied. Are historical details explained if they are not familiar? Do the historical details enhance the storyline?

- **Ways to Relate**
  Can you identify with the main character? Does the story show that even though times change, people are fundamentally the same? Are there insights applicable to our own times?

Back in Time

Writing historical fiction can be very difficult. Not only must the historical setting and details be factual, but the storyline must be stronger than the history. Because this is a challenge, a multi-step scaffold is offered to the students.

Step One
- Students research historical events for the setting of their stories. Using the questions on the next page, have students research information for events in history that interest them. You may want to brainstorm ideas with your class, such as:
  - **Discoveries**—electricity, telephone, light bulb, automobile
  - **American Civil War**—slavery, Underground Railroad, Civil War, politics
  - **Explorations**—Vikings, Columbus, Lewis and Clark, Admiral Byrd
  - **Wars**—French Revolution, World War II, Vietnam, Gulf War
  - **Frontier Life**—Oregon Trail, survival, gold rush, Oklahoma land rush
  - **Disasters**—Pompeii, Titanic, Chernobyl, hurricanes, earthquakes
  - **Important events in world history, national history, and local history**

Step Two
- Students create fictional storylines within their historical settings. A storyline organizer is provided on page 80 to help students record their ideas for the historical fiction piece. This separate plan allows students to delineate the real and fictional portions of their own stories while learning how historical fiction stories are created.

Step Three
- Students combine fact and fiction to draft their own historical fiction stories. When the drafts are complete, meet with each student to help add historical details to his or her story. Explain that they will use factual information about the event as well as fictional events. Sometimes it is easier for students to write the story in the first person, as if they were there, rather than creating a third-person storyline.

Step Four
- Share and enjoy the stories. After sharing, ask questions such as, "What did you learn about history from this story? Have you ever felt the way your character did?"

Historical Fiction Data Sheet

1. Where does your story take place? _____

2. When does your story take place? _____

3. What historical event was happening at that time? _____

_____

_____

4. What type of clothing did people wear?

Men and boys _____

Women and girls _____

5. What were houses like back then? _____

_____

_____

6. Did they have electricity? _____

7. Did they have indoor plumbing? _____

8. What types of transportation did they have? _____

9. What types of jobs did people have? _____

_____

_____

10. List some interesting facts about life at that time. _____

_____

_____

_____

11. Would you like to live during this time? Why or why not? _____

_____

_____

12. What happened as a result of the historical event in the book? _____

_____

_____

Historical Fiction Story Plan

1. Setting of the story _____

2. Historical event _____

3. Who is telling the story? _____

4. Describe the main character. _____

_____

_____

5. What is the relationship between the main character and the historical event?

_____

_____

6. Are there any actual historical people in your story?_____

If so, who? _____

7. Tell about the other characters in your story.

_____

_____

8. What is the main character's problem in the beginning of your story?

_____

_____

9. What happens in the middle of your story?

_____

_____

10. How is the problem solved at the end?

_____

_____

Folktales and Fairy Tales

Folktales and fairy tales are stories that people share with friends and family generation after generation.

Folktales ...

- are stories that have been shared orally and passed down for generations.
- are often fairy tales, a category that includes actual stories about fairies, but also stories that use traditional folktale plots and elements. Two offshoots of this category are modern fairy tales, stories that have been made up, not passed down; and "fractured" fairy tales, which offer parodies of traditional tales and their themes.
- are stories with generic settings, often beginning "once upon a time" and "long ago and far away."
- are stories in black and white, with characters that represent either good or evil (the wicked witch, the good prince, the bad wolf). Characters tend to be flat and not described in detail, such as "the wise old woman" or "the happy king."
- feature main characters who are often alone or isolated in some way, such as Little Red Riding Hood, Hansel and Gretel, or Cinderella.
- often feature a problem that has a life or death outcome.
- reward good and punish evil. These tales often have a "happily ever after" ending.

How to Tell if It's Any Good

Folktales are rich in what they offer you as a reader—wishes come true, imagination is encouraged, recurring symbols are introduced. Folktales allow you to deal with issues that your parents and teachers often avoid, such as one child being loved more than another, death, or danger. You see that main characters are rewarded after hard struggles, both physical and emotional. An example of an excellent folktale should include:

- **Oral Quality**
  Does the story sound like something that was told orally? Is the story full of action? Is there enough repetition to allow for easy memorization?

- **Original Language**
  Is the version as close to the original as possible? Is the version rich in language and not watered down in action? Does the tale offer clues as to its culture or country of origin?

- **Ways to Relate**
  Can the child identify with the hero or heroine? Does the tale inspire hope and courage?

Enriching the Experience

Drama

- Have students work in small groups to create a "new" folktale. Have them perform the tale, using props they've made on their own. Videotape the performance to view at a later time, with the class watching for the elements of a folktale.
- Play "oral" charades with your students. Have students make up quotes that their favorite character might have said, such as, "Now let's see if this glass slipper fits," for the Prince in Cinderella. Encourage students to act out the line with accents, gestures, and feeling.
- Cut out symbols for the elements of folktales. Read a story to the class. Have students raise a symbol whenever they hear one of the elements; for example, raise a number three when hearing a magic number, a smiling face for a good character, or a frowning face for a bad character.

Research and Writing

- Country of Origin
  Read a folktale that offers significant clues to its country of origin. Have students write down clues, then research the answer. This activity could also conclude with a game of "Name My Country."
- Modern Folktales
  Have your students read a modern folktale, such as *The Emperor and the Kite* by Jane Yolen. What elements are missing? Write a whole-class modern folktale using traditional folktale elements and adding contemporary detail.
- Compare and Contrast
  Read two or three versions of a folktale from different countries or cultures. Ask students to find the similarities and differences between them. Then, have students find and read versions on their own. Ask them to write the elements of a folktale for each as a scaffold. Afterwards, students can share lesser-known versions and compare them to tales they know well.

Examples (these are all versions of Cinderella):
Tattercoats by Joseph Jacobs (English)
The Rough-face Girl by Rafe Martin (Algonquin Indian)
The Golden Sandal by Rebecca Hickox (Iraqi)
The Talking Eggs by Robert D. San Souci (American South)

0-7424-1954-1 *Complete Library Skills*

Fantasy Land

When you read a **fantasy** book, you depart reality for a short time and go on a magical journey or you experience an exciting, out-of-this-world event.

A fantasy ...
- includes something that cannot really happen.
- can include an imaginary world.
- offers the reader's imagination an escape from reality and freedom.
- offers the reader a message for living in today's world.

In high fantasy ...
- a fantastical world, such as Oz or Narnia, is presented.
- time is flexible; real-world time is non-existent.
- the main character believes his or her experiences are real.
- the central conflict is between good and evil.

In science fiction ...
- the fantasy is based on scientific theories and technological inventions.
- there are often moral and ethical questions.
- the setting is often in the future.

How to Tell if It's Any Good

All stories can be treasures, but fantasy books allow students the chance to escape this world and visit that wonderful place we call imagination, where anything is possible. Coleridge, writing about poetry, said that fantasy requires the "willing suspension of disbelief." When reading exceptional fantasy, we willingly follow and believe, and the journey enriches us. An example of an excellent fantasy story should include:

- **A Mechanism for Helping You Believe**
  Does the author establish the story in reality before taking us to another world, such as Oz, or does the story start in the alternate world? Does the author give details so believable that we accept them, as in *Charlotte's Web*? Does the author offer created documentation such as pretend news articles or official-sounding notices, as in *Jumanji*?

- **Fairness to the Reader**
  Is the story original, not a copycat of another story? Does it offer fresh and delightful inventions or language? Is the story world consistent throughout the book?

- **Ways to Relate**
  Can the reader identify with the character(s)? Does the story provide some universal truth or wisdom that can be applied to our lives in the real world?

83

Imagine That!

Writing fantasy is a great way to set a child's imagination free. There are many methods for writing a fantasy story, from making an animal speak to creating a whole imaginative world. The setting can be the element that is not real; the characters can be made up, altered, or endowed with special powers; and the events can be those things that cannot really happen. Students may explore any or all of these techniques to create fantasy fiction.

Step One
- Students create a plan using the Fantasy Story Plan on page 85. Brainstorming and drawing offer students opportunities to create ideas. Review the fantastical elements from books shared in class as springboards. Offer the class plenty of time to create and recreate their own fantasy ideas.

Step Two
- Students use their plans to write their fantasy stories.

Step Three
- Students add adjectives and vivid verbs in the revision stage. Dig deeper into a student's imagination to enhance the story if someone is struggling. Have students work in teams for the final editing of stories.

Step Four
- Share the fantasy stories during class time. A wonderful way to share fantasy stories, whether read or written, is to allow students to dress up as characters from their own stories. This allows the imagination to go beyond the written page. A note to send home is included below.

Dear Parents,
As part of our study of genres of literature, your child will be sharing his or her fantasy story with the class. Please allow your child to bring a costume to class so he or she can dress up as his or her favorite character from the story. The costumes should not be elaborate or expensive, only creative and fun for your child.

Thank you for your support in our study of fantasy books!

Sharing Day: _____

Fantasy Story Plan

I. Where and when does your story take place (setting)?

_____

_____

2. Is this a real setting? _____

If not, explain how the readers will know.

_____

3. Tell about the main character of your story.

_____

_____

4. Tell about your other characters.

_____

_____

5. What is the problem in the story?

_____

_____

6. What happens in the middle of your story?

_____

_____

7. How is the problem solved?

_____

_____

8. What events in your story could not happen in real life?

_____

Name _____ Date _____

Informational Books

Books that teach us and inspire us to learn more are called **Informational** books.

Informational books ...
- are filled with information and facts related to a specific topic.
- use content-specific vocabulary.
- use imagery and figurative language to compare the known to the unknown.
- have a specific format including some or all of the following: table of contents, picture or diagram captions, subheadings, sidebars, glossary, index, and bibliography.

Combination books ...
- are fictional storylines used as a means of presenting true information. A popular example of this is the *Magic School Bus* series by Joanna Cole. These books provide information to children in an interesting and exciting manner by combining fiction and factual information.

How to Tell if It's Any Good

Informational books satisfy your sense of wonder and curiosity. You are often inspired to learn more after reading an informational book. Reading informational books also helps you to understand how to read other factual writing found in magazines, newspapers, and other reference materials. An example of an excellent informational book should include:

- **Accurate Facts**
  Is the information correct? Is the information up to date? What are the qualifications of the author to write this book? It's important to learn to check both the copyright dates and the author notes to help assess the book's value.

- **Fairness**
  Is it easy to tell the difference between facts and opinions? Does the author share opposing theories or ideas? Are any significant details omitted? Are stereotypes avoided in both text and illustration?

- **Ways to Relate**
  Does the book answer questions you would ask? Is the information presented in an understandable, organized manner? Is the writing clear and understandable?

Research

- To teach different resource mediums, ask students to look for their specific topics in newspapers, magazines, encyclopedias, dictionaries, and online. Have them compare the types of information each resource offers about the topic.
- Divide the class into groups of four. Require that the students in each group work together to find an answer to a question that you provide, using whatever resources are available.
  Sample question: In Greek mythology, who was the goddess of beauty?
- Have students read how-to books and then try out the instructions. This is a great opportunity to get parents involved. Be certain that your students get approval before beginning this project, as some books may not be appropriate for safety reasons.

Presentation

- Allow students time to find the most effective and creative ways in which to present their information to the class. Ideas include: demonstrations, dioramas, posters, working models, mobiles, computer presentations, flow charts, compare/contrast discussions.
- Give students the opportunity to create a "What do you know?" challenge. This is a fun activity for students because they are the ones who create the test. Students begin by locating fascinating facts about their topics. Next, each student writes a question that can be answered with that fact. Using the question, they will write three other possible answers which all sound plausible. Teach students how to write their questions in multiple-choice format.

Example:
    A narwhal's horn is really
        a. a radar device like bats have.
        b. a tooth grown through the lip.
        c. a hollow tube that makes sounds.
        d. a tool to kill prey.
    Answer: b. a tooth grown through the lip.

Allow the class to take the test after you combine everyone's questions into one format. After the test, allow each student to provide the correct answer to his or her question. Encourage students to supply additional information, too.

Students can also make a book by writing each question on a separate page and then illustrating the answer on the next page.

Poetry

Poetry explores the beauty of language.

Poetry ...
- uses rhythm in words, phrases, and lines, often creating a musical effect.
- can rhyme or be free verse.
- plays with language, sounds, meanings, etc.
- is often written in stanzas, or groups of lines.
- uses economy of words; offers the essence, not the whole thing.
- uses figurative language such as similes, metaphors, and personification.
- uses imagery; the poet paints a picture in the reader's mind.
- can evoke strong feelings and emotions; is powerful.
- leaves the reader with something to think about; is memorable.

Verse ...
- generally has rhyme and rhythm.
- offers little or no depth of emotion.
- does not leave the reader with an important thought or lingering emotion.
- provides poetry readiness.

How to Tell if It's Any Good

Traditionally, poetry has offered human beings an outlet for strong emotions. Poetry also explores the beauty of the language. Children's poetry is a bridge between verse and adult poetry, a journey from simple rhymes to powerful words and ideas. An example of an excellent children's poem should include:

- **Elements That Have Child-Appeal**
  Poems that rhyme and have strong rhythm are fun, but don't be afraid to try other forms of poems, as well. The important thing about choosing a poem is that you choose one that you will enjoy and understand.

- **Beauty of Language**
  The poems you choose should offer vivid imagery—you should be able to picture exactly what the poet is writing about. Words should be precise and meaningful. Figurative language can be difficult to understand, so be careful when choosing a poem that uses this type of language.

- **Ways to Relate**
  Familiar experiences can aid understanding of a poem. Good poetry offers you a way to experience your own feelings, rather than dictating the feelings or beliefs of the poet.

Try Five-Line Poetry Forms

- **Limerick**

  A limerick is a silly or humorous five-line poem. The first, second, and fifth lines rhyme and have three accented beats. The third and fourth rhyme and have two accented beats.

  Examples: (Beat is underlined)

  There <u>was</u> a young <u>man</u> named <u>Pike</u>,
  Who <u>thought</u> he would <u>go</u> for a <u>hike</u>,
  But he was too <u>weak</u>
  To get to the <u>peak</u>
  He <u>wished</u> he'd re<u>mem</u>bered his <u>bike</u>.

  A <u>brave</u> young <u>scout</u> from the <u>North</u>,
  When <u>asked</u> if <u>he'd</u> venture <u>forth</u>,
  Stepped <u>ahead</u> of the <u>rest</u>
  And <u>puffed</u> out his <u>chest</u>
  Then <u>answered</u> in <u>lisp</u>, "Of <u>courth</u>!"

Write several limericks as a class so students understand the rhythm and rhyming pattern. Then let them try some on their own. Share them as a class.

- **Cinquain**

  A cinquain is also a five-line poem, but it does not rhyme. The traditional cinquain is based on syllables: two, four, six, eight, and two syllables in the five lines, respectively. A variation of this type of cinquain is one in which parts of speech are used to set the pattern instead.

  Line 1: a noun
  Line 2: two adjectives
  Line 3: three verbs ending in "ing"
  Line 4: a phrase about the noun
  Line 5: a synonym for the noun

  snow
  cold, wet
  scooping, packing, throwing
  my little sister running away
  snowballs!

  Other examples:

  kittens
  pouncy, fluffy
  playing, sleeping, clawing
  curled up in your lap
  friends

  summer
  warm, fun
  swimming, running, jumping
  ice cream dripping down my hand
  freedom

  *Limericks and cinquains by N. Robert Hatfield

This form of poetry uses the students' knowledge of the parts of speech. Write several cinquains together or allow students to create their own. Have a contest for the most creative topic and words.

Suggested Poetry List

The following is a list of recommended poems to use when introducing poetry to your students:

TITLE AND AUTHOR	Rhythm Word Music	Rhyme	Plays with Language	Stanzas	Economy of Words	Figurative Language or Imagery	Strong Feelings	Something to Think About
"The Pickety Fence" by David McCord	●	●	●			●		●
"Eight-Oh-Three" by Carol Diggory Shields	●	●	●			●		
"There Was an Old Man with a Beard" by Edward Lear	●	●		●	●	●		
"Have You Ever Seen?" (Anonymous)	●	●	●					●
"Smokescreen" by Charles Ghinga	●	●	●	●	●	●		
"The Swing" by Robert Lois Stevenson	●	●		●	●	●	●	●
"The Creature in the Classroom" by Jack Prelutsky	●	●			●	●		
"Jimmy Jet and His TV Set" by Shel Silverstein	●	●		●	●	●		●
"Mummy Slept Late and Daddy Fixed Breakfast" by John Ciardi	●	●		●	●	●		
"Fog" by Carl Sandburg					●	●		
"America the Beautiful" by Katharine Lee Bates	●	●		●	●	●	●	●
"Who Has Seen the Wind?" by Christina Rossetti	●	●		●	●	●		
"Since Hanna Moved Away" by Judith Viorst	●	●		●	●	●	●	●
"Four Little Foxes" by Lew Sarett	●	●		●	●	●	●	●
"Slithergadee" by Shel Silverstein	●	●	●		●	●		
"Mother Doesn't Want a Dog" by Judith Viorst	●	●		●	●	●		●
"Fueled" by Marcie Hans	●				●	●		●

Name _____ Date _____

So Many Choices!

When you use a library for research, you have many options of places to look for information—encyclopedias, almanacs, atlases, nonfiction books, magazines, and the Internet. Each type of book is different and so you would choose to use them for different reasons. The web shows you the types of books you can use for researching a topic and the differences between the books. Keep in mind that many subjects can be found using any or all of the research materials listed in the web.

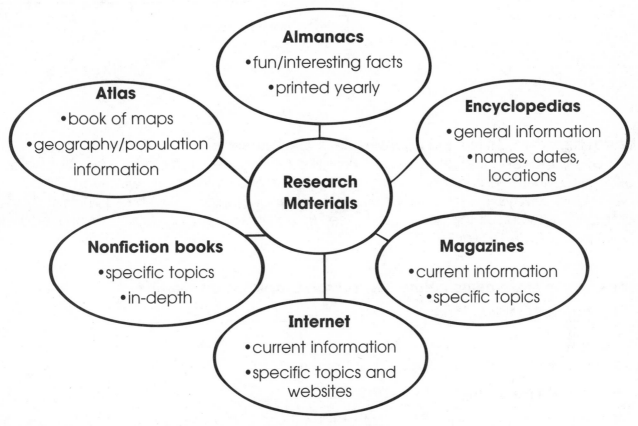

▶ **Answer the questions about reference materials.**

1. If you wanted to learn about tidal waves, what sources could you use?

_____

2. What is one advantage of using a magazine to obtain information?

_____

3. Why might you choose to use a nonfiction book about the Milky Way Galaxy instead of using an encyclopedia article?

_____

4. If you are using an atlas, what kind of information are you looking for?

_____

Name _____ Date _____

Fact or Opinion?

When taking notes, you should learn to identify facts from opinions. There are key words you should look for when reading that will tell you that an opinion is being stated. Look at a few of these key words.

Opinion Words	
I think …	favorite
I believe …	always, never
I feel …	best, worst

Words like *I think, I feel,* and *I believe* describe how someone feels about something. Not everyone feels the same way. Words like *always, never, favorite,* and *worst* are exclusive. Most things in the world cannot be described factually with words like *never* and *always.* These usually describe personal opinions. When reading facts and opinions, ask yourself this: *Which of these statements does not change from person to person, or place to place?*

► **Look at the statements below. Write *fact* or *opinion* on the line.**

 1. Earth is the third planet from the sun. _____

 2. Earth is round. _____

 3. Earth is the most beautiful planet in the universe. _____

 4. I have a pet named Buster. _____

 5. He is the cutest dog in the neighborhood. _____

 6. He is better behaved than my friend's dog. _____

► **Read a news story in a newspaper. On a separate sheet of paper, take notes based on the factual information in the article. Then read an editorial from the same newspaper. Write down all the opinions you find. Highlight the key words and phrases that make you think they are opinions. What differences do you notice between these two articles?**

Note Taking

It is important to know how to take good notes when you are using information from a book. Taking good, precise notes can save you a lot of time when doing research for a paper or a report. You only want to record information that is important to your topic. Writing down unnecessary facts and information can slow down your research and can get in the way of creating an A+ report. When taking notes from reference material, keep the following tips in mind:

- First read headings, subheadings, and summaries. Review questions that may appear at the end of the chapter. Note sidebars that contain highlighted information. Look at pictures and any captions that appear underneath.
- Don't write exactly what you read. Be accurate, but write your notes in abbreviated form and in your own words.
- Write as clearly as possible and leave some room in the left margin for comments.
- When you are finished, review your notes and highlight the most important information.
- Look for answers to the questions *Who?*, *What?*, *Where?*, *When?*, *Why?*, and *How?*

Mapping

For some students, taking detailed notes may be a distraction from the text. If you are distracted when trying to take notes on lined paper, the answer for you may be mapping. This is a graphic organizer. First write the main idea of your text in a circle in the center of the page. Then write supporting details around the main idea. This process of note taking allows you to see the relationships between supporting details and the main idea. Look at the example below.

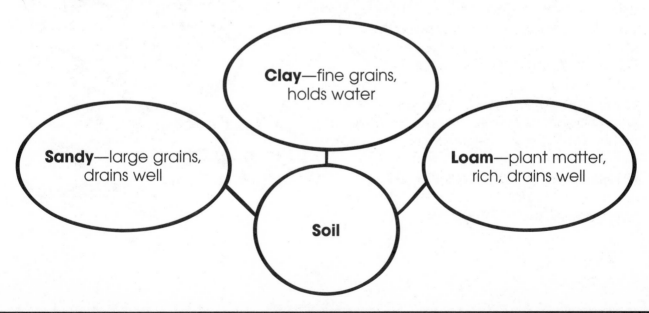

Using Note Cards

Note cards are a handy, convenient way to take notes. It is helpful to use one note card per idea to help keep your notes neat and straight. Label the top of each note card with a heading that quickly tells you what information the note card contains.

➤ **Read the information below from a chapter book. Underline the main idea. Take notes on the note cards on the next page.**

Animals have often led the way for human explorers. The journey into space is no different. The first animals to survive a trip into near space were a monkey and 11 mice on a United States *Aerobee* sounding rocket in the early 1950s. They rode straight up and then down again.

Russian space dog, Laika, is thought of as the first true space traveler from Earth. Laika in Russian means *barker*. In 1957, she was the only passenger aboard the Soviet spacecraft *Sputnik 2*. Laika survived for ten days in orbit, but she died before the craft crashed back to Earth.

The first living creatures to survive a controlled ride on an American craft were Able and Baker, a pair of squirrel monkeys. They rode in a capsule atop a *Jupiter C* rocket in 1959. A chimp named Ham is the official holder of the title "first chimpanzee on a U.S. space flight." He made his journey in 1961. He trained for his space flight by learning to pull certain levers when he saw flashing lights. Each time he chose the correct lever he was rewarded with a banana pellet. The space capsule he was in landed in the ocean, and almost sank. But Ham was pulled to safety. Another chimp, Enos, was the first American animal to orbit Earth. He made two circuits and returned alive.

Note Cards

Try to use a new note card for each new idea.

Angel's Adventure

➤ Read chapter one of the story below. Take notes on the notes sheet on the next page.

Brandon scratched the tip of his nose. It always itched when something was wrong, and now it was itching like crazy. He pushed open the back door to his house and stepped inside the kitchen.

"Mom," he called.

No answer. He looked up at the corkboard on the wall near the refrigerator—grocery list, receipt for the cleaners, picture of his pet rat, Angel—but no note. Brandon checked the house and finally threw his backpack on the bed in his upstairs bedroom.

"I wish she'd tell me if she isn't going to be home," Brandon complained to Angel, who was clinging, upside down, from the top of her cage. He opened the cage door and let the chubby white and brown rodent scurry across his desk. The phone on the desk rang, causing Angel to leap for safety onto Brandon's shoulder and down the back of his shirt.

"Hello?" Brandon smiled when he heard his best friend's voice. "What's up, Christina?" he asked.

"I'm really steamed," his friend replied. "My mom was supposed to take me to the mall today to get my ears pierced. She promised me if I got an A on my book report we would go."

"Oh, and she's backing out?" asked Brandon sympathetically.

"No, she's not even here!" Brandon's nose itched again. "My sister is gone, too."

Christina's sister, Courtney, had just graduated from college and was living at home while she looked for a job. She was a lot older than Christina, but she was always willing to give her sister a ride when she needed it.

"Hold on a sec," Brandon said. A droning noise outside had caught his attention. He pushed the curtains aside and looked down into his neighbor's yard. His classmate, Jon, stood on the back steps staring at the lawnmower. It was running by itself, turning in lazy circles around a concrete birdbath in the center of the yard. Jon took a few steps, caught the machine by the handle, and turned it off. He glanced around, then looked up and saw Brandon at the open window.

"Have you seen my dad?" he called. Brandon shook his head no.

"Brandon? Are you there?" Christina's voice called through the phone.

Brandon looked up and down the street. There wasn't a single car on the road. "Let me call you back," he answered, puzzled. He replaced the phone on its cradle and scratched the end of his nose.

Notes Sheet

▶ **Fill out the notes sheet using information from the chapter on page 96.**

◯	**Characters**
	Setting
	Conflict
◯	**Important Plot Events**
	Supporting Details
	What I Think Will Happen in the Next Few Chapters
◯	

Name _____ Date _____

Outlining

An **outline** is a skeleton of a story, speech, report, or text. It is used to organize your notes. There are certain rules you have to follow when creating an outline.

- **Main Ideas** are noted with Roman numerals (I, II, III, etc.) followed by a period. Each main idea begins with a capital letter.
- **Subpoints** are indented and are noted with capital letters (A., B., C., etc.) followed by a period. Each subpoint begins with a capital letter.
- **Supporting details** are indented and noted with numerals (1., 2., 3., etc.) followed by a period. Each detail begins with a capital letter. Further details are noted with lowercase letters (a., b., c., etc.) followed by a period.

There are two main types of traditional outlines:

- A **topic-only outline** is written in brief, simple phrases. There aren't periods after each phrase.
- A **sentence outline** is written in detailed, complete sentences, which may be used as topic sentences for paragraphs. Words or sentences in equal positions should be of equal importance.

▶ **Look at the topic-only outline below:**

   I. Birds
      A. Pelicans
      B. Penguins
         1. Emperor penguins
         2. King penguins
         3. Macaroni penguins
  II. Mammals
      A. Dogs
         1. Golden retrievers
         2. Beagles
      B. Cats
 III. Reptiles
      A. Lizards
      B. Snakes

Name _____   Date _____

Venture to Venus

▶ **Read the article below. Circle the main ideas. Underline the subtopics. Then create an outline on the next page using that information.**

Venus is the second planet from the sun. It is slightly smaller than Earth, with a diameter of about 7,500 miles.

Volcanic eruptions have covered much of the surface with lava flows. It is a barren planet with huge plains and lowlands. There are two important highland areas—Aphrodite Terra, which is about the size of Africa; and Ishtar Terra, similar in size to Australia. The highest point on Venus is in the Maxwell Montes on Ishtar. It includes a peak that soars seven miles above the surface.

The atmosphere of Venus is made up mostly of carbon dioxide. It acts like a blanket to keep in heat, and the temperatures can reach 900 degrees Fahrenheit—that is hot enough to melt lead! Atmospheric pressure at the surface of the planet is 90 times greater than that of Earth. Venus is covered with a layer of clouds of surfuric acid, which lead to acid rain. Most of this probably evaporates in the extreme heat before it reaches the surface.

Venus spins in the opposite direction of Earth. That means that on Venus, the sun rises in the west and sets in the east. It spins very slowly, taking 243 Earth days to complete one full turn on its axis. Since Venus completes one orbit around the sun in 225 Earth days, a day on Venus is longer than its year.

Name _____ Date _____

Venture to Venus Outline

Title _____

I. Main idea _____

   A. Subtopic _____

      1. Subtopic detail _____

      2. Subtopic detail _____

   B. Subtopic _____

      1. Subtopic detail _____

      2. Subtopic detail _____

II. Main idea _____

   A. Subtopic _____

      1. Subtopic detail _____

      2. Subtopic detail _____

   B. Subtopic _____

      1. Subtopic detail _____

      2. Subtopic detail _____

III. Main idea _____

   A. Subtopic _____

      1. Subtopic detail _____

      2. Subtopic detail _____

   B. Subtopic _____

      1. Subtopic detail _____

      2. Subtopic detail _____

   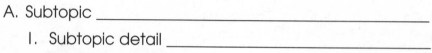 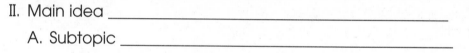

A Walk in the Park

Atlases feature many different kinds of maps. Chances are that you'll have to use a map to find information someday. It is important to know how to use the maps in an atlas.

▶ **Look at the map of the park below. Write directions from Ted's house to the water park. Write your directions on the lines below.**

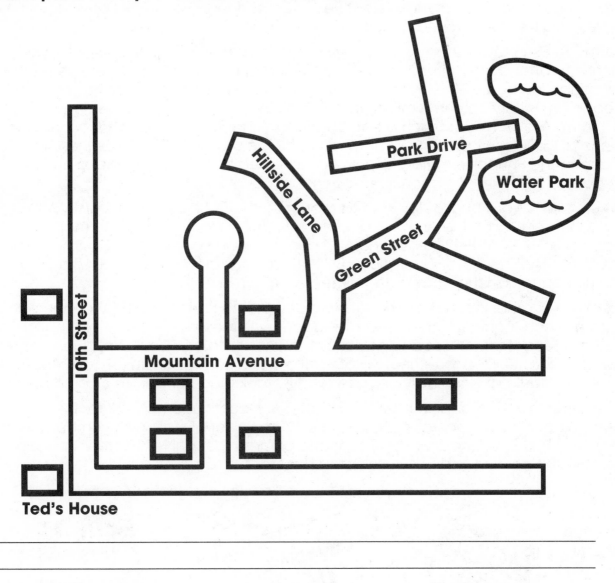

Park Drive

Hillside Lane

Water Park

Green Street

10th Street

Mountain Avenue

Ted's House

_____

_____

_____

_____

💡 **Tip!** Use sequence words such as first, then, next, last, finally, before, and after. Or you may want to number your directions in the correct order.

I Like Ike

▶ **Read the following article. Answer the questions on the next page to summarize what you have read.**

Dwight David Eisenhower, whose real name was David Dwight Eisenhower, was born in Texas in 1890. Besides being the 34th President of the United States, Eisenhower had an incredible military career. More than thirty years of military experience prepared him for his two terms (eight years) as President. He was well-respected by citizens and leaders around the world.

Although Eisenhower's family believed in practicing peace, he was encouraged by friends to attend the military academy at West Point in New York, where he received his education and military training. After graduation in 1915, "Ike," as he was called, began his military career, moving up from second lieutenant to first lieutenant in the U.S. Army. He worked for such great leaders as Brigadier General Fox Conner and General Douglas MacArthur. While working for MacArthur in the Philippines, he planned the Philippine military defense and helped in putting together a military academy for their newly formed independent country.

When World War II began, Ike earned a promotion to brigadier general. By March 1942, after serving in the Army's war plan division, he was promoted to major general. In June of 1942, he was named commanding general of the U.S. forces in the European Theater of Operations. By 1943, Ike was promoted to four-star general, the highest rank in the Army at that time.

His military career impressed the leaders of the United States and he was named supreme commander of the Allied Expeditionary Forces in Europe. In this position, he made sure that the armies and navies of the United States, Great Britain, and other Allied nations worked together to protect the world from German invasion. The infamous battle at Normandy on June 6, 1944, took place under Ike's command.

Even after the German surrender in May 1945, Ike continued his work for the U.S. Army. As a five-star general, he was named Army chief of staff in November 1945. In 1950, Ike was given the position of supreme commander of NATO forces in Europe. He held this position until he was elected President.

I Like Ike (cont.)

➤ Answer the questions below about the article on page 102.

1. Briefly summarize Eisenhower's military career. Write facts in sequential order, according to the article.

_____

_____

_____

_____

2. List six different military positions Eisenhower held in the United States Army.

_____

_____

_____

3. Using the dates given in the article, make a timeline below showing the progress of Eisenhower's military career.

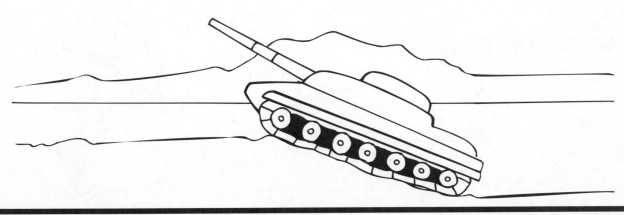

Name _____ Date _____

Researching an Invention

Your teacher has assigned the following research project for you:

_____

Invention

▶ **Using the graphic organizer below, take notes on your assigned invention. Use multiple research materials. Add more legs to the map if needed. Then use this information to write a report on the invention you researched.**

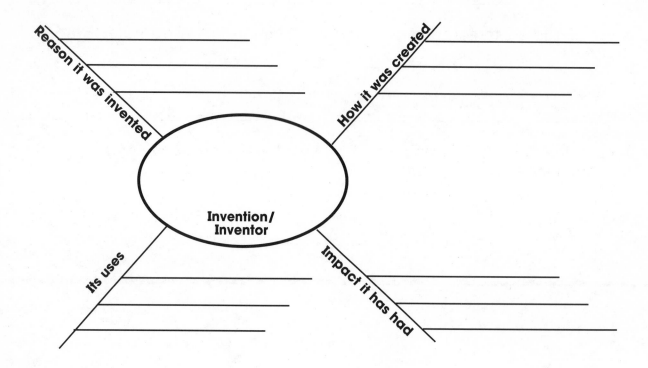

Reason it was invented

How it was created

Invention/ Inventor

Its uses

Impact it has had

Bibliography of research materials

_____

_____

_____

 **Researching Two Cities**

▶ **Compare and contrast two cities in the United States. Research each city's climate, size, population, location, food, activities, etc. Use multiple reference materials. Take notes in the Venn diagram below, using one circle for each city and the overlapping area for their similarities. Make sure you label each circle. Use this information to write a report on how the two cities are similar and how they are different.**

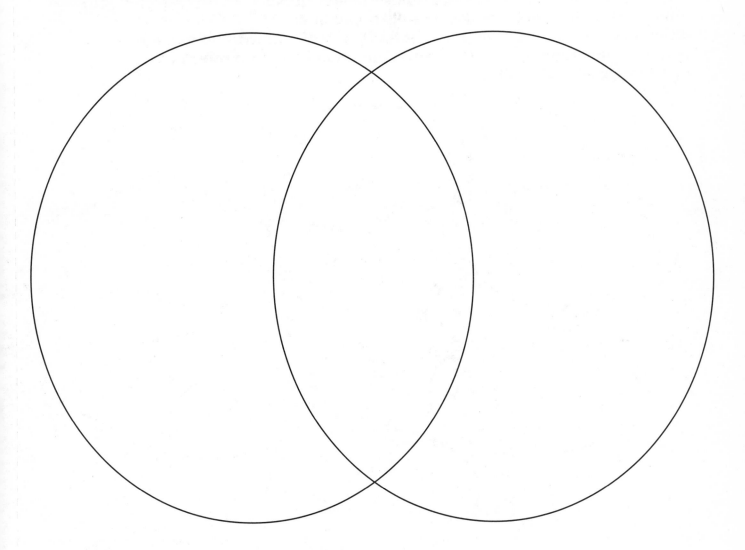

Bibliography of research materials

_____

_____

_____

 0-7424-1954-1 *Complete Library Skills*

Researching an American President

Do you have a favorite American President? Are you interested in learning more about a President that you don't know much about? Now's your chance to do so.

► **Choose a President that you want to research. Use many reference materials. Take notes in the graphic organizer below. Write the President's name in the center circle and the important information that you want to include in the surrounding circles. Use this information to write a report about the President you've chosen.**

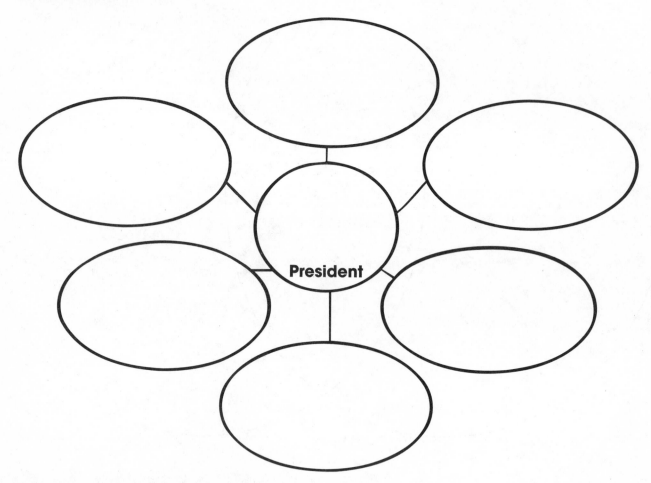

President

Bibliography of research materials

_____

_____

_____

Name _____ Date _____

The Electronic Card Catalog

Electronic card catalogs can be searched by subject, title, author, keyword, or call number. The information that is found on a card from the card catalog drawer can also be found in the results of an electronic search. Look at the results from an electronic search below.

> **581**
> **BLA** **Title**: Plants—The World of Science.
> **Author**: Black, David.
> **Published**: New York: Facts on File Publications, 1984.
> **Description**: 64 p.: col. ill.
> **Notes**: Includes glossary and index.
> **Notes**: A readable, scientific introduction to the world of plants.
> **Elec. Access**: Internet sites about Plants.
> **Subject**: Science—Dictionaries.
> **Subject**: Plants.

▶ **Answer the questions about the catalog card above.**

1. What is this book about? _____

2. Who is the author? _____

3. What is this book's call number? _____

4. If you did a subject search for this book, what subjects would you look under?

   _____

5. When was this book published? _____

   Where was it published? _____

Boolean Searches

When doing an online search, there are words you can use to help you get the results you want. The words *AND, OR,* and *BUT NOT* are called **Boolean operators**. Using these words in a keyword search will help you get fewer, more exact results that are closer to your topic. Look at the example below:

Search for: | Michigan **AND** Great Lakes

⦿ AND   ◯ OR   ◯ BUT NOT

Michigan **AND** Great Lakes—your results would only mention both Michigan and Great Lakes.

Search for: | Michigan **OR** Great Lakes

◯ AND   ⦿ OR   ◯ BUT NOT

Michigan **OR** Great Lakes—your results would mention Michigan, Great Lakes, and both.

Search for: | Michigan **BUT NOT** Great Lakes

◯ AND   ◯ OR   ⦿ BUT NOT

Michigan **BUT NOT** Great Lakes—your results would only mention Michigan.

▶ **Using your library's online catalog, do the following search.**

Search for: | asteroids **AND** space

⦿ AND   ◯ OR   ◯ BUT NOT

1. Using **AND** as a Boolean operator, did you get many results? _____

▶ **Now refine your search and use *OR* instead of *AND* for a Boolean operator.**

2. How have your results changes? _____

3. Why do you think your results changed so much? _____

4. How did you use a Boolean operator to find the information you needed?

_____

Little Words, Big Results

Using Boolean operators (AND, OR, BUT NOT) can really affect the results of a search. It is a good idea to use them often so you get the best search results possible.

▶ **Use the following criteria to search on your library's electronic card catalog. Then answer the questions.**

Search for: | World War II **BUT NOT** Germany |

○ AND   ○ OR   ● BUT NOT

1. What do you notice about the results of your search?

_____

2. Write ten book titles that appear in your results.

_____   _____

_____   _____

_____   _____

_____   _____

_____   _____

▶ **Now let's change your search by using a different Boolean operator.**

Search for: | World War II **AND** Germany |

● AND   ○ OR   ○ BUT NOT

3. How have the results of your search changed?

_____

4. What can you conclude about using Boolean operators?

_____

_____

_____

_____

Name _____ Date _____

Searching by Title

When you know the title of the book you want but don't know where to find it in the library, do a title search. When you perform a title search, you can leave off the words *the*, *a*, and *an*. These words are unnecessary.

▶ **Your best friend recommended a book to you. She knows the title, but doesn't know the author. So you do a title search together. Look at the results below. Answer the questions.**

Title Search	the bad beginning

1. Are there any unnecessary words in the entry? _____

   If so, what are they? _____

2. Does it matter if you use capital letters when doing a search? Try it! _____

▶ **Here are the results of your search. Answer the questions that follow.**

Number	Title	Year
1	The Bad Beginning (A Series of Unfortunate Events/Lemony Snicket) Illustrated by Brett Helquist	2003
2	The Bad Beginning (A Series of Unfortunate Events) (videorecording) LDS Publications, Ltd.	2003
3	The Bad Beginning (A Series of Unfortunate Events)/Lemony Snicket	2003

3. The book she recommended to you has illustrations, so which result should you choose? _____

4. What would you find on the bookshelf if you chose result number 2?

   _____

5. If you wanted to search for this book by the author, what would you enter into an author search? _____

6. What is the call number of this fiction book? _____

Searching by Author

You want to find a book by one of your favorite authors—Patricia MacLachlan. Hmm… you entered Patricia MacLachlan into the author search and no records were found. The browser asks for **last name first**, so you retype her name. Several books come up and you select the one you are most interested in—*Sarah, Plain and Tall*.

▶ **Below is the record that came up on the computer screen. Use it to answer the questions below.**

> **F**
> **MAC**   **Author** MacLachlan, Patricia
> **Title**   Sarah, Plain and Tall
> **Pub Info**   New York: Charlotte Zolotow Book, c1985.
> **Description**   58 p.
> **Summary**   When their father invites a mail order bride to come live with them in their prairie home, Caleb and Anna are captivated by their new mother and hope that she will stay.
> **Subject**   Stepmother—fiction
> **Subject**   Frontier and pioneer life—fiction
> **Subject**   Newbery medal
> **Subject**   Historical fiction

1. What year was the book published? _____
2. What is the book's call number? _____
3. How many pages are in the book? _____
4. Who is the publisher of the book? In what city is the publisher located?

   _____

5. Would this book be helpful in doing a report on pioneer life? Explain.

   _____

6. For what subject searches would this book be a result?

   _____

7. Has this book won any medals? _____ If so, which medal? _____

8. What would you enter for a title search for this book? _____

   What would you enter for a call number search for this book? _____

Name _____ Date _____

Searching by Subject

You have always wanted to go on a hot air balloon ride. There's only one problem—you're incredibly scared of heights! One of your teachers told you that the way to overcome a fear is to face it head on. So you do a subject search to find some books on hot air balloons. Here is what comes up on your computer screen.

Number	Subjects (1–5 of 5)	Entries Found
1	Hot Air Balloons	11
2	How Hot Air Balloons Work	4
3	Fear of Heights	2
4	Hot Air Balloon Designs	8
5	Hot Air Balloon Noise Recording	1

 Answer the questions about the results above.

1. Which of the results is the most general? _____

2. Which results would help you overcome your fear? _____

3. To better understand hot air balloons, which results should you choose?

_____

 You choose to read about fear of heights, so you select subject number 3. Look at the books under this subject. Answer the questions about these books.

Subject	Fear of Heights

Number	Title (1–2 of 2)	Year
1	Don't Look Down!	2003
2	Overcoming Your Fears	2002

4. Which book focuses specifically on a fear of heights? _____

5. What do you think you would find inside *Overcoming Your Fears*? _____

_____

Searching by Keywords

Outer space has always fascinated you. You want to find books on outer space exploration, but you're not sure which type of search would be better—a subject search or a keyword search. So you try it both ways.

The keyword search returned over 100 records! Ugh! The subject search returned over 50 records! Still too many! You remember that you can use Boolean operators to help narrow down your search, so this time you type *outer space AND exploration*. Ah-ha! A list of only eight titles comes up. Much better!

▶ **Answer the questions below about your searches.**

1. Which appears to be more accurate, a subject search or a keyword search?

   _____

2. Why did using the word *AND* between two keywords help you find what you were looking for? _____

3. What do you think would have happened if you entered *outer space BUT NOT exploration*? _____

4. A keyword search looks over the entire record for a word, but a subject search only looks in the subject headings for the word. When might a keyword search be more helpful? When might a subject search be more helpful? Explain.

   _____

   _____

▶ **Perform your own keyword searches using the topics below. First search by keyword for the word in bold print. Then search using a Boolean operator with the word that follows it. Write your observations of the two searches on the line.**

5. Keyword—**weather** AND tornadoes

   _____

6. Keyword—**dogs** OR animals

   _____

Using the Internet

The Internet is a great place to look for information on any topic. Many times, you can find all the information you need for a report using the Internet. You just need to know how to search and where to look so that you are using high-quality, accurate information.

Many websites are not qualified to present the information that is found on their websites. These are the websites you want to stay away from. But how do you know which websites are reliable and accurate and which ones are not? Look at the chart below. These are a few things to notice when considering whether or not to use the information from a website.

Reliable Sources

- no typing mistakes
- easy to read and understand; graphics are clear and add to the content of the site
- include in-depth information
- not biased; contain objective facts
- updated often; current information
- from a reliable source; you've heard of the organization that created the page (a URL ending with **.gov**, **.edu**, or **.org** is also a good sign)
- stable; the pages stick around for a long time and are always there when you go back to them

Not-so-reliable Sources

- contain typing mistakes
- difficult to read; graphics are distracting
- information is not in-depth or accurate
- it only shows one person's opinions
- page hasn't been updated in a long time
- you've never heard of the organization that created the page
- here today, gone tomorrow; page is not there when you look for it a few months later

Where Should I Look?

Read the assignments below. Decide which website would be the best site to use to find the information you need. Circle the right choice. Then write why you chose that site on the line.

1. You are doing a presentation on a fairy tale. You need to learn about how it originated, where it originated, any hidden meanings behind it, and different versions of it. Which website should you choose?

   a. My Favorite Fairy Tales
     http://www.myfairytales.com/Jenni/littleredridinghood
   b. The History of Fairy Tales
     http://www.um.edu/english/fairytales/history
   c. Cinderella
     http://www.cinderella.com/buy

_____

2. You are creating a model that works with a pulley. You want to learn more about how a pulley works before you start building your model. Which website should you choose?

   a. Simple Machines
     http://www.simplemachines.org/pulley
   b. Harvey's Hardward
     http://www.harveyshardware.com/pulley/sale
   c. Build Your Own Model
     http://www.makeamodel.com/blueprints

_____

3. You are doing a report on your favorite breed of dog—the spaniel. Which website should you choose?

   a. Dog Days
     http://www.dogdays.com/subscription
   b. Spaniels Rock
     http://www.spanielsrock.com/picturesofRocky/Ben
   c. Dog Breeds Around the World
     http://www.dogbreeds.org/spaniels/facts

_____

Can You Spot the Good Website?

1. You want to learn about different types of weather. Which of the computer screens below looks more factual? Circle your answer and explain why you chose it.

a.

◄ ► ⊗ ↺ [_____] Go

Weather
■ Types of Storms
■ Types of Clouds
■ The Weather in Pictures
■ Storms of the Century
■ Safety Tips

Ⓗ   Ⓛ

last updated April 2004

b.

◄ ► ⊗ ↺ [_____] Go

Wether! Wether! Wether!
△ Click here! To see how a tornadoe works
△ I love rain storms
△ What is your favorite type of weather? Readers share their stories.

last updated May 1997

_____

_____

- -

2. Websites contain a lot of valuable information on general topics, such as animals, books, math, and much more. Search the web for some of these sites. Write the addresses and topics below and keep this list for future reference.

Website Address	Topic
_____	_____
_____	_____
_____	_____
_____	_____
_____	_____

Name _____ Date _____

Work or Play?

The Internet is both fun and educational. Some websites are good to use when you need to collect facts for a project or report. Other websites are just for fun.

▶ **Read the address of each website below. Write what you think can be found on each website on the line next to it. Then, using a search engine, find another website on the same topic. Write the website address on the blank line and a description of what the site contains.**

Cooking

1. http://www.chefsaroundtheworld.org _____

2. http://www.cookierecipes.com/sugar/decorate _____

3. http://www.cookbooks.com/grilling/buy _____

4. _____ _____

Literature

5. http://www.juvenilefiction.com/authors/silverstein _____

6. http://www.umich.edu/poetry/haiku _____

7. http://www.booksnmore.com/cart/checkout _____

8. _____ _____

Flip Fact Book

Students will research a nonfiction topic of their choice and then construct layered flip books. They will also create library card catalog entries, summarizing the facts shared in their books. Each summary card gives you a quick way to verify the student's overall understanding of his or her topic.

Materials Needed
You will need to provide three brad fasteners for each student. You may also want to provide paper in different sizes than those specified, to ensure the books are uniform in size. Another option is to set a minimum and maximum page size to allow for more creativity on the part of your students and greater variety of flip fact books.

Introducing the Project
Take time to show examples of the various ways that layered pages are used. Show examples of picture books, pamphlets, and brochures to help students better visualize their own books.

When visiting your school library, have students examine a card catalog and note the type of information and location of information on the cards. If your library's card catalog is electronic, you may want your students to design their cards according to the electronic format. Have the media specialist discuss the importance of the card catalog. You can also show students a file box where you plan to store their catalog cards in alphabetical order. These steps will help students see the real-life applications for this component of the project.

Classroom Connections
Read a nonfiction selection to students and then brainstorm facts and opinions from the reading. You can turn this into a game by organizing the class into two teams. Call on a student from one team to make a statement, such as, "Angelfish are the most beautiful fish of all." Then challenge the other team to identify this as a fact or an opinion.

Ask someone from a professional field, such as law, medicine, journalism, or publishing, to talk to the class about whether fact or opinion plays more of a part in his or her daily work.

Flip Fact Book

Genre: Nonfiction

Due Date: _____

Dear Fourth Grader,
Discovering new facts about an exciting nonfiction topic is so much fun! For this project, you will do research on a subject of your choice. You will use your findings to create your own Flip Fact book to share in our classroom.

Materials Needed
You will need three brad fasteners given to you in class; markers, crayons, or colored pencils; and five sheets of $8\frac{1}{2}$" x 11" paper. You will also need notes from your research to write about four amazing facts.

Project Requirements
1. Leave one of your $8\frac{1}{2}$" x 11" sheets of paper as it is. Measure and cut the other four sheets to these sizes: 7" x 11", $5\frac{1}{2}$" x 11", 4 " x 11", and $2\frac{1}{2}$" x 11".
2. The shortest piece of paper will be your cover. Stack the other sheets of paper as shown. Once you have them in the right order, ask someone to help you hold them firmly together as you punch three holes across the top of the cover.

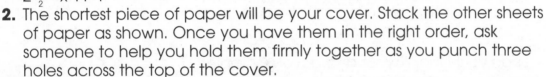

3. Separate your pages and begin planning your layout. Your cover will have a title which clearly indicates the topic you researched, your name as author, and a picture to illustrate your topic.

4. The other four pages of your book will present four amazing facts that you found during your research. At the bottom of each page will be a sentence that leads to the next page of the book. Your most amazing fact will be on the back cover.

Plan your writing so that each page ends with these lead statements:
4" x 11" page—You won't believe it, but …
$5\frac{1}{2}$ " x 11" page—I was amazed to learn that …
7" x 11" page—Did you know that …
$8\frac{1}{2}$ " x 11" page—The most surprising fact I
                      discovered was …

5. Write a rough draft before you copy your report onto your Flip Fact book.
6. Assemble your finished book using the brad fasteners through the holes.
7. Use the card catalog format to write a description of your Flip Fact book on a 3" x 5" index card.
8. Fill in the Project Designer's tag on page 121. Tape it to the back of the book.

Here's Your Schedule for the Flip-Fact Book Project:

Check Box When Completed

Week 1—Have your topic approved by your teacher. Select the books you want to use. Begin reading and collecting information.

☐

Week 2—Continue reading and taking notes. Cut out your book pages. Start writing rough drafts of pages.

☐

Week 3—Design your book layout and cover. Complete book by copying information onto the pages. Assemble book using the brad fasteners.

☐

Week 4—Write rough draft of card catalog entry. Copy onto a 3" x 5" card.

☐

Flip Fact Book

How did your book project go? Are you happy with the results? Did you enjoy learning more about the topic that you chose?

▶ **Evaluate how you did by filling in the chart below.**

Criteria	Excellent	Good	Fair	Needs Improvement
My written work is well-organized, neat, and accurate.				
I used a high-quality source for my information.				
My illustrations are a result of my best effort.				
I thoroughly read about my topic and took many notes.				
My project completely meets project requirements.				

Project was turned in on time. ☐ Yes ☐ No

Project Designer's Tag

Name _____

Date _____

Topic _____

Types of research materials used

_____

_____

Newbery and Caldecott Book Award Winners

The following lists highlight the last 15 years of Newbery and Caldecott award winners:

Newbery Award Winners

2003: *Crispin: The Cross* of Lead by Avi
2002: *A Single Shard* by Park, Linda Sue
2001: *A Year Down Yonder* by Peck, Richard
2000: *Bud, Not Buddy* by Curtis, Christopher Paul
1999: *Holes* by Sachar, Louis
1998: *Out of the Dust* by Hesse, Karen
1997: *The View from Saturday* by Konigsburg, E. L.
1996: *The Midwife's Apprentice* by Cushman, Karen
1995: *Walk Two Moons* by Creech, Sharon
1994: *The Giver* by Lowry, Lois
1993: *Missing May* by Rylant, Cynthia
1992: *Shiloh* by Naylor, Phyllis Reynolds
1991: *Maniac Magee* by Spinelli, Jerry
1990: *Number the Stars* by Lowry, Lois
1989: *Joyful Noise: Poems for Two Voices* by Fleischman, Paul

Caldecott Award Winners

2003: *My Friend Rabbit* by Rohmann, Eric
2002: *The Three Pigs* by Wiesner, David
2001: *So You Want to Be President?* by Small, David
2000: *Joseph Had a Little Overcoat* by Taback, Simms
1999: *Snowflake Bentley* by Azarian, Mary
1998: *Rapunzel* by Zelinsky, Paul O.
1997: *Golem* by Wisniewski, David
1996: *Officer Buckle and Gloria* by Rathmann, Peggy
1995: *Smoky Night* by Diaz, David
1994: *Grandfather's Journey* by Say, Allen
1993: *Mirette on the High Wire* by McCully, Emily Arnold
1992: *Tuesday* by Wiesner, David
1991: *Black and White* by Macaulay, David
1990: *Lon Po Po: A Red-Riding Hood Story from China* by Young, Ed
1989: *Song and Dance Man* by Gammell, Stephen

Artemis Fowl: The Eternity Code by Colfer, Eoin

Babe the Gallant Pig by King-Smith, Dick

Because of Winn-Dixie by Dicamillo, Kate

Boxcar Children # 1 by Warner, Gertrude Chandler

Bunnicula by Howe, Deborah and James

Charlotte's Web by White, E. B.

Dear Mr. Henshaw by Cleary, Beverly

Frindle by Clements, Andrew

From the Mixed Up Files of Mrs. Basil by Konigsburg, E. L.

Fudge-A-Mania by Blume, Judy

Hank the Cowdog 01 The Original Adventures by Erickson, John R.

Harriet the Spy by Fitzhugh, Louise

Harry Potter and the Chamber of Secrets by Rowling, J. K.

Harry Potter and the Sorcerer's Stone by Rowling, J. K.

Island of the Blue Dolphins by O'Dell, Scott

James and the Giant Peach, Dahl, Roald

Lenny and Mel by Kraft, Erik

Lily's Crossing by Giff, Patricia

Little House in the Big Woods by Wilder, Laura Ingalls

Martin's Mice by King-Smith, Dick

Mary on Horseback by Wells, Rosemary

Number the Stars by Lowry, Lois

Ozma of Oz by Baum, Frank L.

Poppy by Avi

Ragweed by Avi

Sammy Keyes and the Hotel Thief by Van Draanen, Wendelin

Stone Fox by Gardiner, John Reynolds

Tales of a Fourth Grade Nothing by Blume, Judy

The Bad Beginning by Snicket, Lemony

The BFG by Dahl, Roald

The Cricket in Times Square by Selden, George

The Houdini Box by Selznick, Brian

The Indian in the Cupboard by Banks, Lynne Reid

The King's Equal by Paterson, Katherine

The Midnight Fox by Byars, Betsy Cromer

The Trouble with Tuck by Taylor, Theodore

The Witches by Dahl, Roald

The Wonderful Flight to the Mushroom Planet by Cameron, Eleanor

almanac—A book filled with fun facts and interesting information. It is printed yearly.

atlas—a book of maps

autobiography—a book that is written by the person it is about

author card—The author card begins with the author's last name. This is the first line on the card.

bibliography—a list of resources that were used for information

biography—A book that is written about someone's life. It is written by someone other than whom the book is about.

book spine—The book spine is the outside edge of the book. It has the call number printed on it. This is what you see when you pull a book from the shelf.

Caldecott Medal—a medal awarded yearly to the artist of the most distinguished American picture book

call number—This can be found on the spine of the book. It shows you where you can find a book in the library. Fiction call numbers start with an *F*. Nonfiction call numbers start with a three-digit prefix.

catalog card—This card shows the author of the book, title of the book, publishing information, copyright date, illustration information, and number of pages in the book. Other information may also be printed on the card.

copyright date—this is the date the book was printed

Dewey Decimal Classification® system—a system of organizing nonfiction books by subject created in 1876 by Melvil Dewey

dictionary—a book of definitions

encyclopedia—a set of books that holds general information on thousands of subjects

fairy tales/folktales—Stories that have been passed down orally from one generation to another. They often feature good versus evil.

fantasy—a story that takes place in an imaginary world and cannot really happen

fiction—make-believe books that are created in the author's imagination

graphic organizer—a type of note-taking format that helps you see relationships between words and facts; webs, charts, Venn diagrams, timelines, etc.

guide words—words found at the top of a page in a reference book to help you find a word you are looking for

historical fiction—a make-believe story that features historical elements, such as the setting or characters

illustrations—pictures and art within a book

informational—books filled with factual information on a specific topic

Internet—a system of networks that connects computers around the world

magazine—A short collection of stories or articles. It is usually published once a month.

Newbery Award—a medal awarded yearly to the author of the most distinguished American story book

nonfiction—Tells a true story. The story is based on facts and can be about many different subjects.

poetry—A written piece that can be silly, serious, sad, funny, etc. Usually rhymes, but doesn't have to.

publisher—The group of people who create a book. They print it and put it together.

realistic fiction—a make-believe story that has the potential of being real

search engine—a software program that searches and gathers information that is about a certain subject

subject—what the book is about

subject card—The subject card begins with the subject of the book. It is shown in capital letters.

table of contents—found at the beginning of a book, it shows you the title of each chapter or page in a book

thesaurus—A book that shows multiple ways to say something. It shows synonyms and antonyms for common, overused words.

title card—The title card begins with the title of a book. This is the first line on the card.

title page—found in the front of a book, this page shows the title, author, illustrator, and publishing information

Answer Key

True or Made-Up? 6
1. fiction
2. fiction
3. nonfiction
4. nonfiction
5. nonfiction
6. nonfiction
7. nonfiction
8. fiction
9. nonfiction
10. nonfiction

Fiction Call Numbers 7
Call number for *Fudge-a-Rama*: Ca
Call number for *My Night on Pluto*: Fa
Call number for *Call of the Wild*: F St

Don't Miss This Call......................8
1. F St
2. F Re
3. F So
4. F Sh
5. F Co
6. F St
7. F Ma
8. F Ti
9. F Bu

Order Up! 9
Books in alphabetical order:
1. F Ba, Todd Bally
2. F Br, Aaron Brody
3. F Cr, Lindsey Crowley
4. F Di, Bob Dilbert
5. F Fi, Jennifer Filey
6. F Hu, Clint Hubbert
7. F Ma, Catherine Marks
8. F Ob, Cho Obo
9. F Ph, Greg Phent
10. F Po, Dan Porter
11. F Ra, Tania Rabinau
12. F Ro, Henry Rolston
13. F Sn, Roger Snider
14. F Wh, Barbara White
15. F Zu, Carrie Zucker

Musical Books...........................10
Beginning: Helen Haward, Adrienne Armor, Brent Buster, Fran Henderson
Middle: Sarah Jackson, Alison Martin, Amy Pilson, Paul Peterson
End: Sherry Thomson, Trent Wilson, Susan White

Arrange the Nonfiction Books........................13
1. 2, 4, 5, 3, 1
2. 3, 5, 4, 2, 1
3. 5, 4, 3, 2, 1
4. 5, 4, 3, 2, 1
5. 2, 4, 5, 1, 3

Whale of a Trail........................14
Correct order of path: 190 Ba, 200 Zu, 240 Aa, 280 Ch, 310 Ew, 330 Th, 350 Tr, 400 Hi, 470 Pu, 470 Va, 520 Cr, 690 Du, 780 Ar, 780 St, 840 Kl, 900 Ma

Understanding the Card Catalog 15
1. subject card
2. title card

Card Catalog Drawers 16
1. fiction
2. Waterbowl, New Jersey
3. 68 pages
4. *The Invisible Dog*
5. Each card has the call number on the top line.
6. subject drawer

Reading a Card......................17
1. F Pl
2. *Nick Nederveld, Ping-Pong Superstar*
3. Pamela Platts
4. New York, New York
5. Volley Press
6. 2003
7. yes
8. It is a story of a ping-pong champion.
9. fiction
10. title card

Reading a Card......................18
1. F Th
2. *The Overprotective Watchdog*
3. Mitch Thompson
4. 80 pages
5. The story of an overprotective dog.
6. Rockville, New Jersey
7. fiction
8. yes
9. 2003
10. Valley Press

Reading a Card......................19
1. *The New Kid*
2. F Fl
3. fiction
4. James Flann
5. 45 pages
6. 2003
7. It is a story of a boy who just moved to a new town.
8. yes
9. Feelings
10. subject card

An Egyptian Journey 22
1. desert
2. pyramid
3. sand
4. ancient
5. pharaoh
Correct order of words in story: pharaoh, ancient, Egyptian, tomb, desert, archaeologists, mummy, treasure, sand, jewels, curse

Snake Eyes...................................23
1. indoor
2. neat
3. soccer
4. copy
5. wig
6. fender
7. orphan
8. push
9. kiss
10. year
11. hunter
12. right
13. prose
14. bass
15. lift
Snake fact—Snakes have no eyelids.

Guide to the Stars.......................24
1. telescope
2. star
3. light
4. sky
5. picture
6. space
7. astronomy

Di•vi•ding Words....................25
tri•an•gle (3)
puz•zle (2)
grape (1)
mil•lion•aire (3)
tel•e•vi•sion (4)
train (1)
a•rith•me•tic (4)
feath•er (2)
can•dle (2)
dol•phin (2)
cat•er•pil•lar (4)
li•on (2)

Decisions, Decisions.................26
1. drag•on•fly
2. dough•nut
3. ra•di•o
4. po•em
5. praise
6. re•spon•si•ble
7. let•ter
8. ox•y•gen
9. jour•nal
10. con•sist•ent
11. de•hy•dra•tion
12. ter•ri•ble
13. av•e•nue
14. un•wind
15. en•deav•or
16. u•ni•form
17. cat•e•go•ry
18. con•scious
19. grand•son
Riddle answer: shrewdness

**What Kind of
Word Is It?**............................27
1. noun
2. adjective
3. adjective
4. verb
5. adjective
6. noun
7. jolt
8. wax
9. pad
10. ebb
11. stray

**Where Does
It Belong?**............................28
Nouns: restaurant, maze, soda
Verbs: keep, decide, flip, publish, carry
Both: produce, match, copy, plant

Multiple Mania.....................29
1. 5
2. 2
3. to shut off from view
4. a line of houses enclosed by streets
Answers will vary.

**Reading Between
the Lines**..............................30
1. outer covering of a tree trunk
2. to tighten or turn
3. parts of a human or animal
4. the side of a river
5. attract

**Where Would
You Look?**............................32
1. Volume 4
2. Volume 11

3. Volume 12
4. Volume 9
5. Volume 12
6. Volume 4
7. Volume 4
8. Volume 1
9. Volume 8
10. Volume 14
11. Volume 4
12. Volume 3
13. Volume 14
14. Volume 8
15. Volume 11
16. Volume 4
17. Volume 7
18. Volume 4
19. Volume 14
20. Volume 4
This set has 14 volumes.

**A Wealth of
Information**..........................33
1. Volume 11
2. Volume 8
3. Volume 1
4. Volume 9
5. Volume 5
6. Volume 4
7. Volume 10
8. Volume 3
9. Volume 11
10. Volume 2
11. Volume 2
12. Volume 11
13. Volume 2
14. Volume 2
15. Volume 14
16. Volume 3
17. Volume 3
18. Volume 11
19. Volume 12
20. Volume 3

Which Word is Key?.................35
1. atomic, Volume 1
2. Democratic, Volume 4
3. Madison, Volume 9
4. North Atlantic Treaty Organization, Volume 10
5. Australia, Volume 1
6. Atlantic Ocean, Volume 1
7. Wisconsin, Volume 14
8. Queen Elizabeth II, Volume 11
9. Newton, Volume 10
10. missiles, Volume 9
11. Appalachian Mountains, Volume 1
12. hockey, Volume 6
13. radio, Volume 12
14. post offices, Volume 11
15. Taft, Volume 13

See Also ... .37
1. travel
2. ships
3. airplanes
4. automobiles
5. airplanes
6. highways or travel
7. ships
8. ships
9. automobiles
10. airplanes
11. ships
12. railroads

**U.S. States
and President**...........................40
Across
4. wheat
5. cardinal
6. Hudson
7. Virginia
8. Taft
9. Oklahoma
10. Rhode Island
Down
1. Nashville
2. Frankfort
3. Raleigh

Facts Online...............................46
World Almanac For Kids
1. Tivoli Gardens
2. A community of living things that depend on each other in a particular place, such as a forest or pond.
3. Leslie King; It was changed when he was adopted by his stepfather named Gerald R. Ford.
4. Igor Sikorsky, 1939
5. Answers will vary.
Farmers Almanac and Old Farmer's Almanac
Answers will vary.

What Is an Atlas?.......................47
Most answers will vary by atlas.

**Finding Your
Way Around**.............................48
Jacksonville—H3
Beardstown—H3
White Hall—I3
Carlinville—J4
Waverly—I4
Hillsboro—J5
Pittsville—I2
Chatham—I4
Granite City—K4

Answer Key

The Magazine Table of Contents 50
1. Nutrition and Baking
2. Baking Cakes
3. Buying the Right Ingredients
4. Baking Special Holiday Treats
5. Learning to Cook: A Guide for Kids
6. Baking Cookies
7. How to Cook Vegetables

Which Magazine Should I Use? 51
1. Weather Magazine
2. Shark and Sea Life Magazine
3. American History for Kids
4. Animals of the Wild
5. Putting on a Play
6. Science Magazine for Kids
7. Insect Digest
8. Rhyme Time Magazine
9. Dog Magazine
10. Whales

Running References 52
Encyclopedia:
The life of King Tut
General information about the Seven Wonders
Chief products of China
Dictionary:
Spelling of *assimilation*
Meaning for the word *faint*
Parts of speech of *smile*
Atlas:
Physical features of India
Location of Venice on a map
Highways through Utah
Almanac:
The weather in Nairobi
Population of Green Bay
Inventor of the toaster
Thesaurus:
Synonyms for *loud*
Antonym for *steady*
Another word for *loyal*

Match the Dewey 65
1. a
2. b
3. j
4. h
5. i
6. d
7. c
8. f
9. e
10. g

Biography Call Numbers 72
1. 921 Ho
2. 921 Dr
3. 921 Fo
4. 921 Re
5. 921 Di
6. 921 Ru
7. 921 Ro
8. 921 Te
9. 921 Wr
10. 921 Ho

Autobiography Call Numbers 73
1. 921 Bo
2. 921 He
3. 921 Ma
4. 921 Ei
5. 921 Ro
6. 921 Da
7. 921 Ha
8. 921 Li
9. 921 Li
10. 921 Wa

Fact or Opinion? 92
1. fact
2. fact
3. opinion
4. fact
5. opinion
6. opinion

Using Note Cards 94
Main idea: Animals have often led the way for human explorers. Notes will vary.

Venture to Venus 99
Main ideas: Volcanic eruptions have covered much of the surface with lava flows.
The atmosphere is made mostly of carbon dioxide.
Venus spins in the opposite direction of Earth.

The Electronic Card Catalog 107
1. It is an introduction to the world of plants.
2. David Black
3. 581 BLA
4. You could search under Science or Plants.
5. 1984; New York

Searching by Title 110
1. yes; the
2. no
3. You should choose number 1.
4. You would find a video.
5. Snicket, Lemony
6. F Sn

Searching by Author 111
1. 1985
2. F MAC
3. 58 pages
4. Charlotte Zolotow Book; New York
5. yes; it includes details about what life was like as a pioneer.
6. Stepmother—fiction; Frontier and pioneer life—fiction; Newbery medal; Historical fiction
7. yes; the Newbery medal
8. Sarah, Plain and Tall; F MAC

Searching by Subject 112
1. Number 1
2. Number 3
3. Number 2
4. Number 1
Answers will vary.

Searching by Keyword 113
1. a subject search
2. The word *and* required the results to have both words in the result.
3. None of the results would have included the word *exploration*.
4. A keyword search is useful when you're not quite sure what you are looking for, but you have an idea. A subject search is useful when you know you want information within a certain subject.

Where Should I Look? 115
1. b
2. a
3. c

Can You Spot the Good Website? 116
1. a
2. Answers will vary.